Ancient Egypt Coloring Book

Color Test Page

Color Test Page

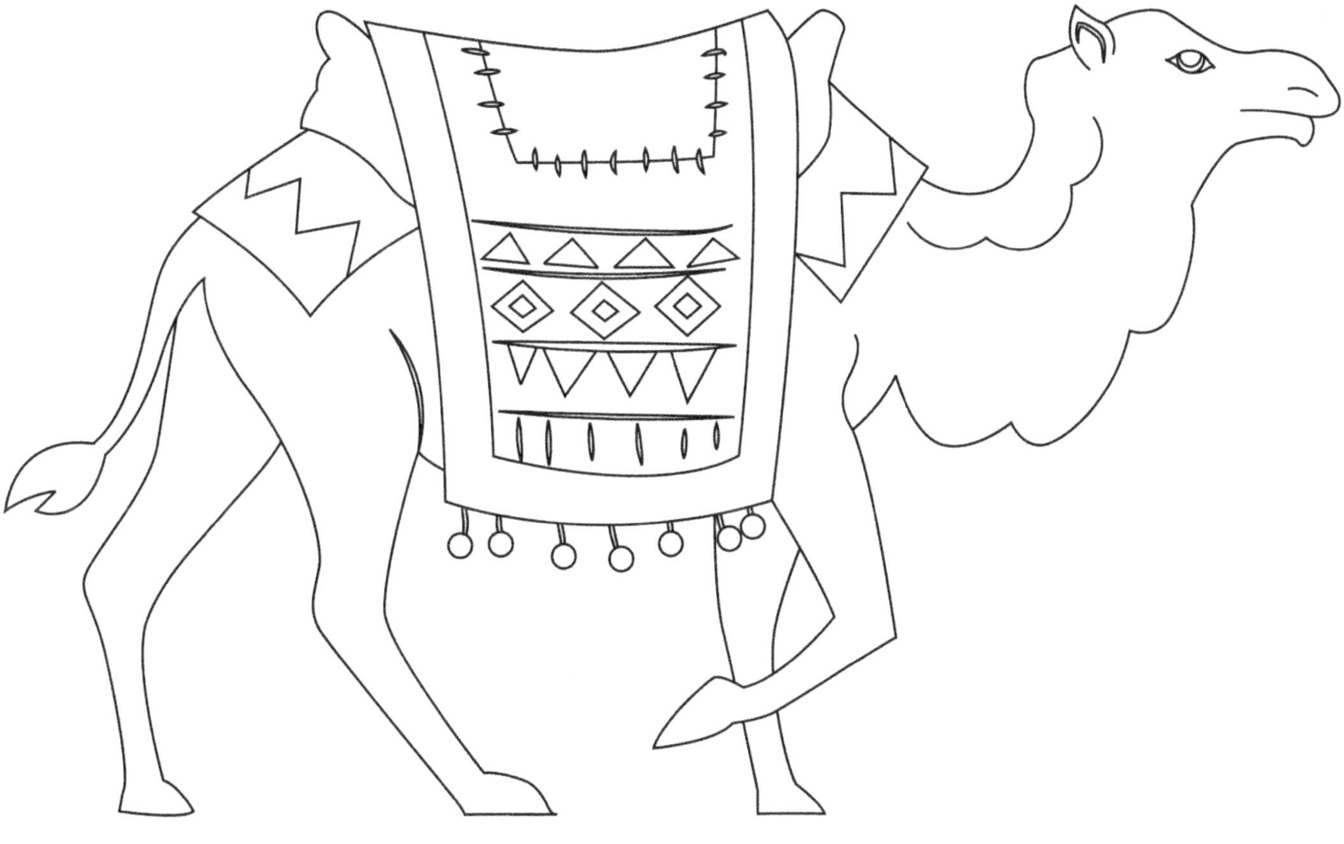

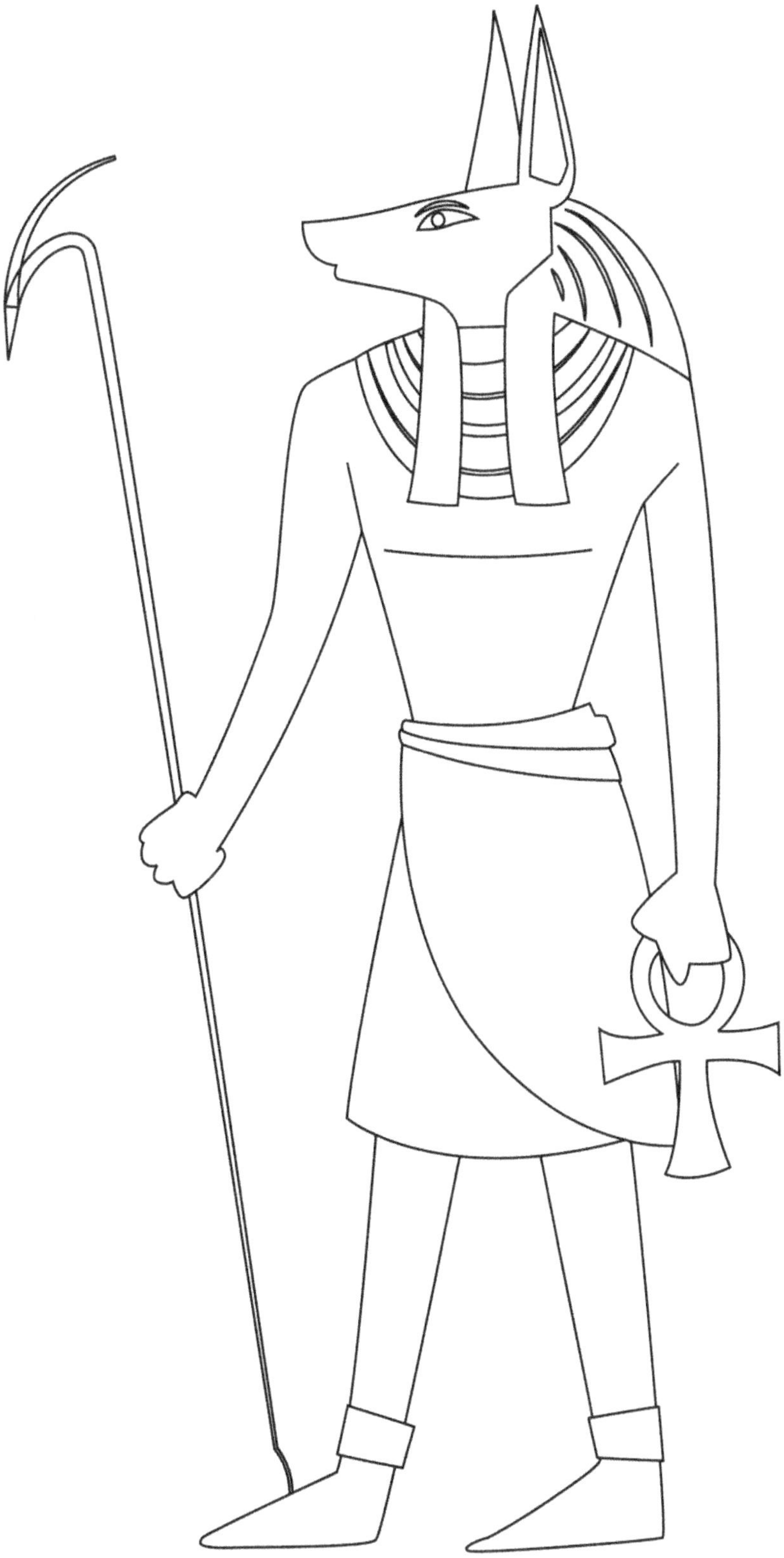

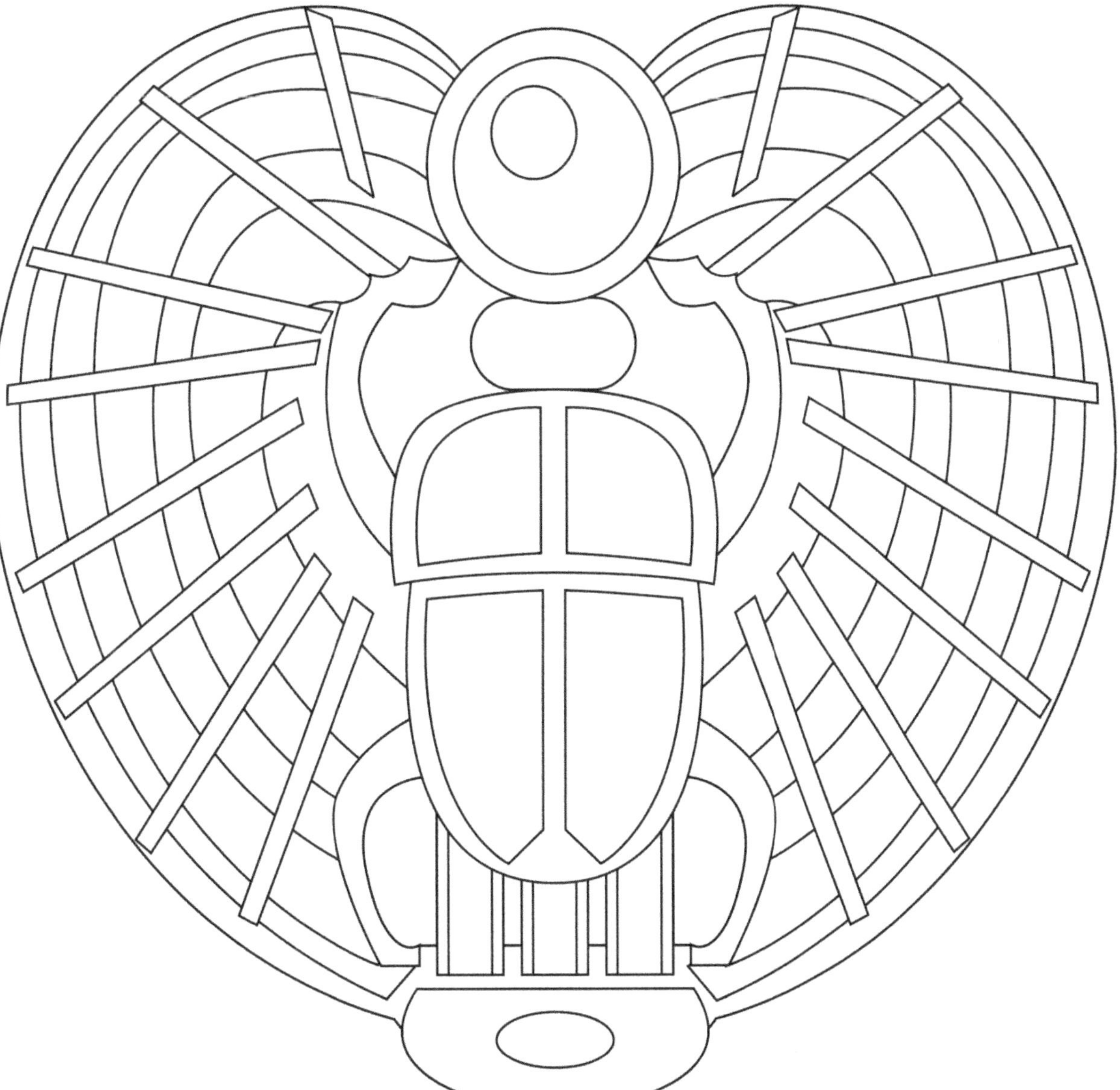

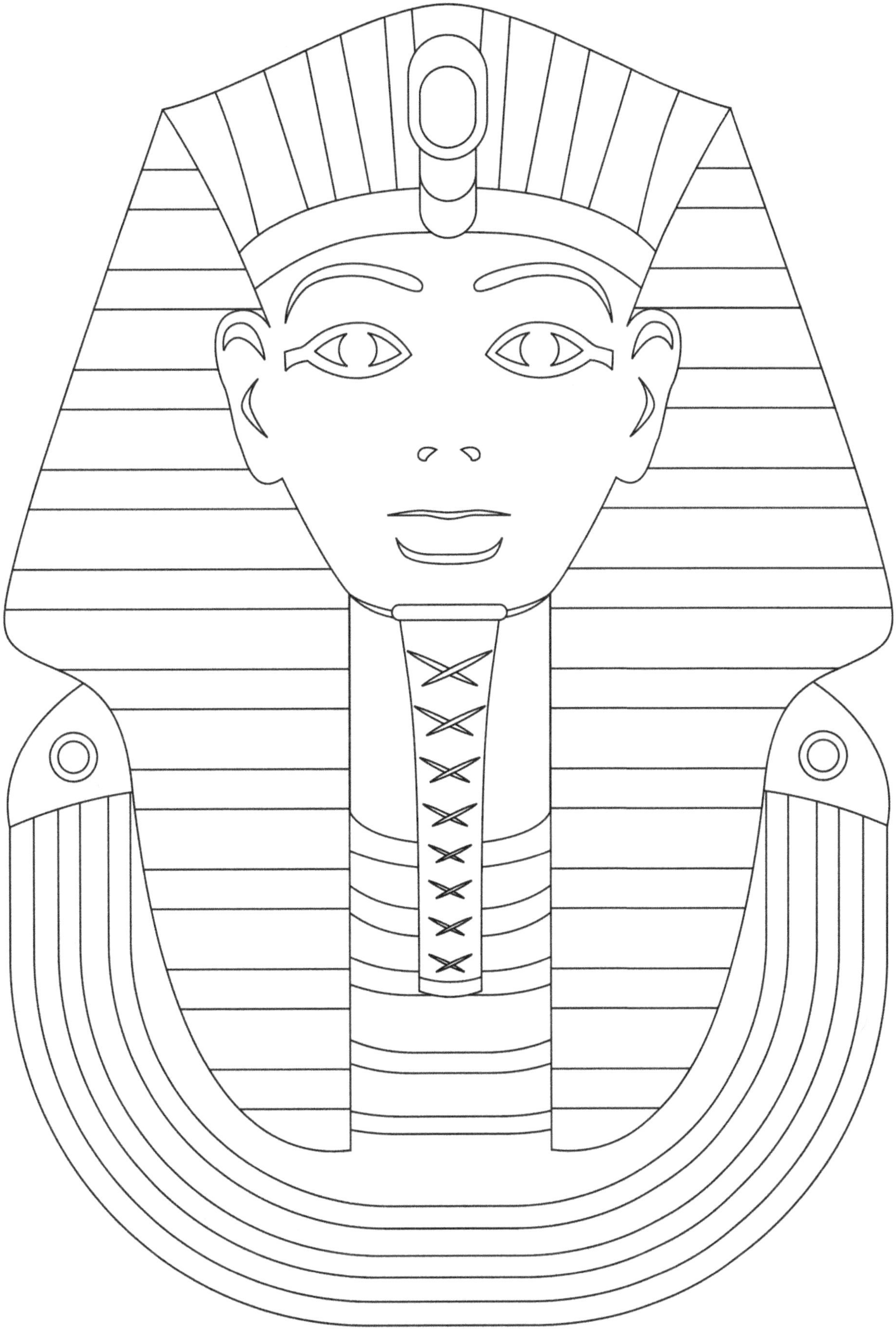

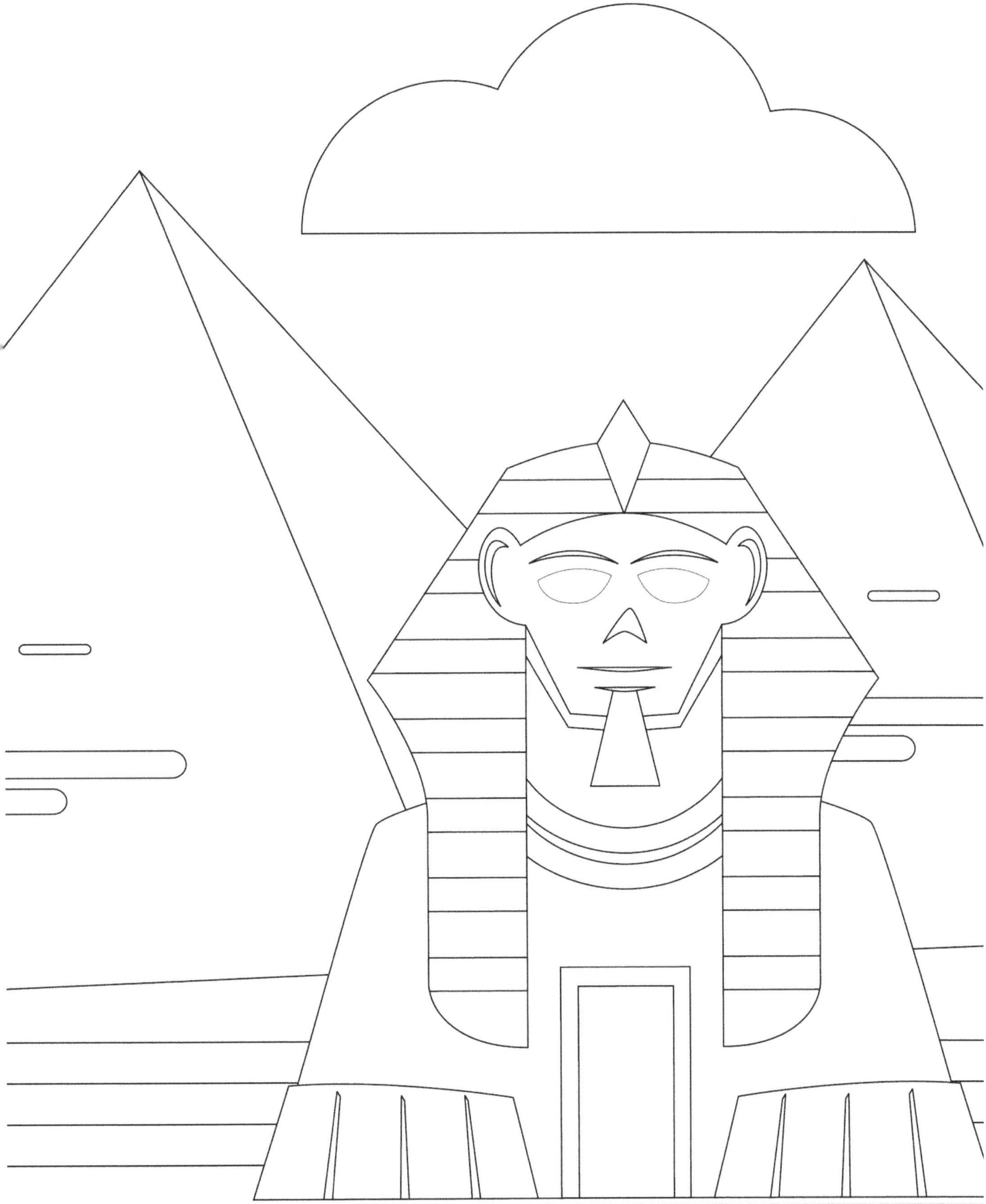

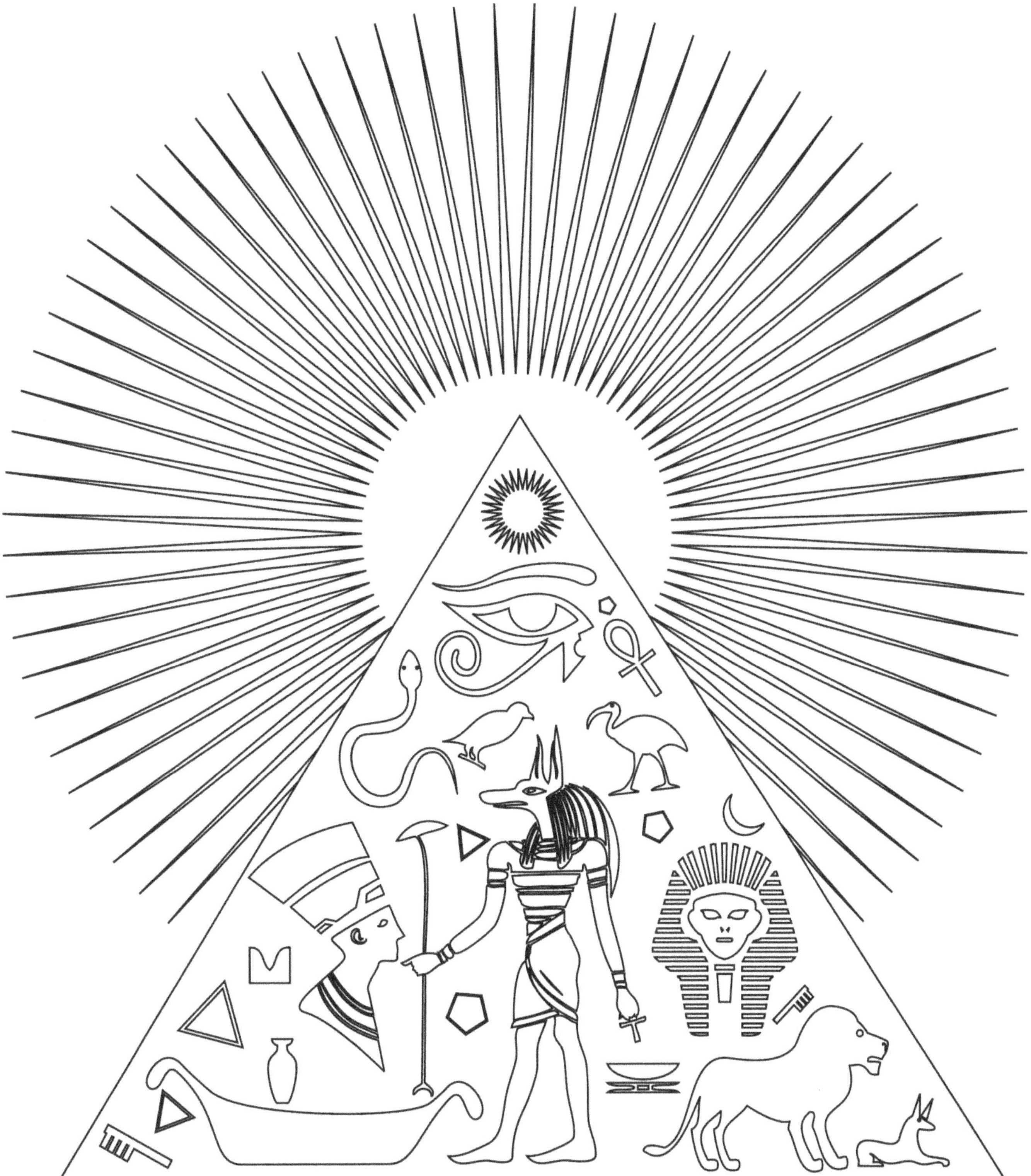

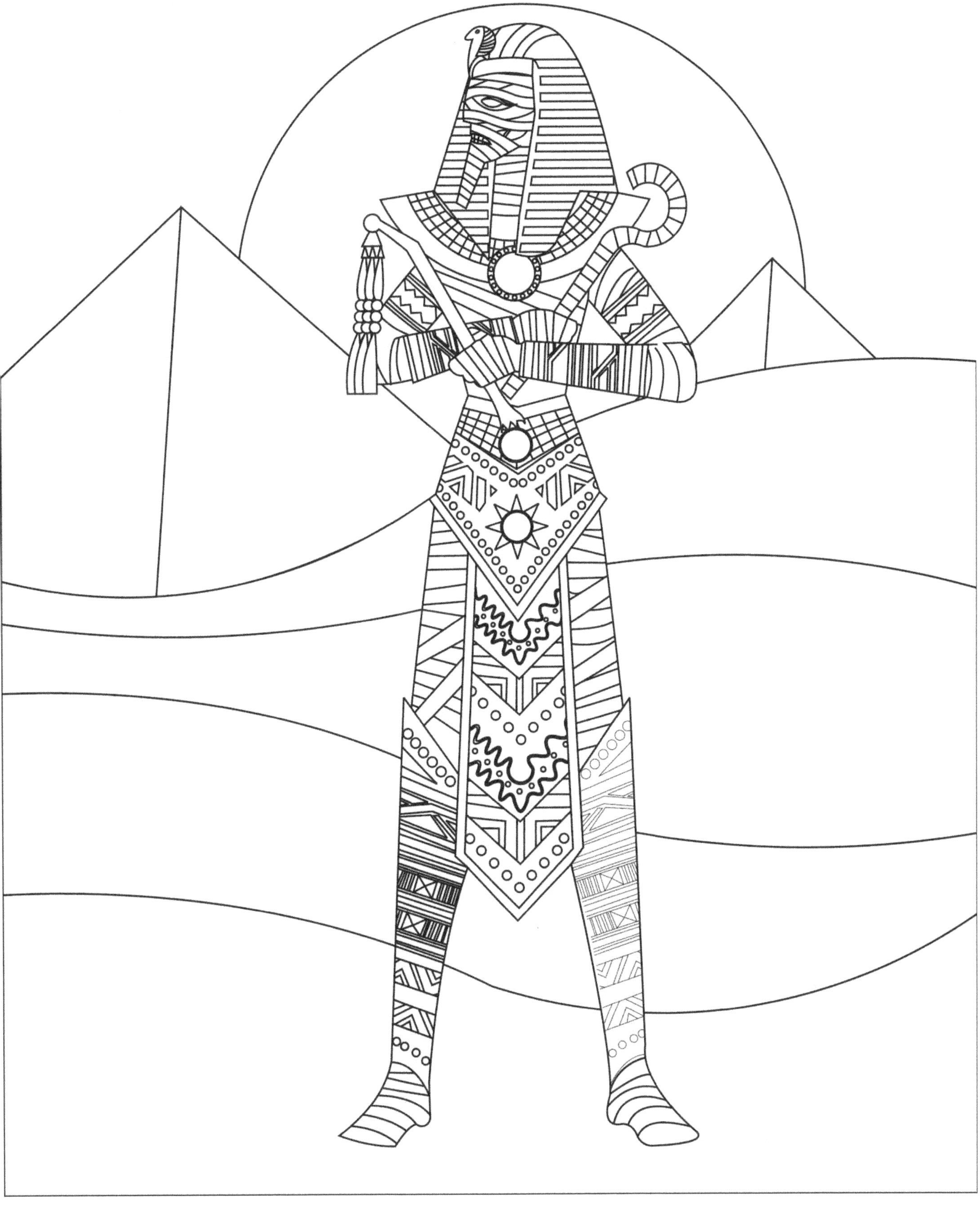

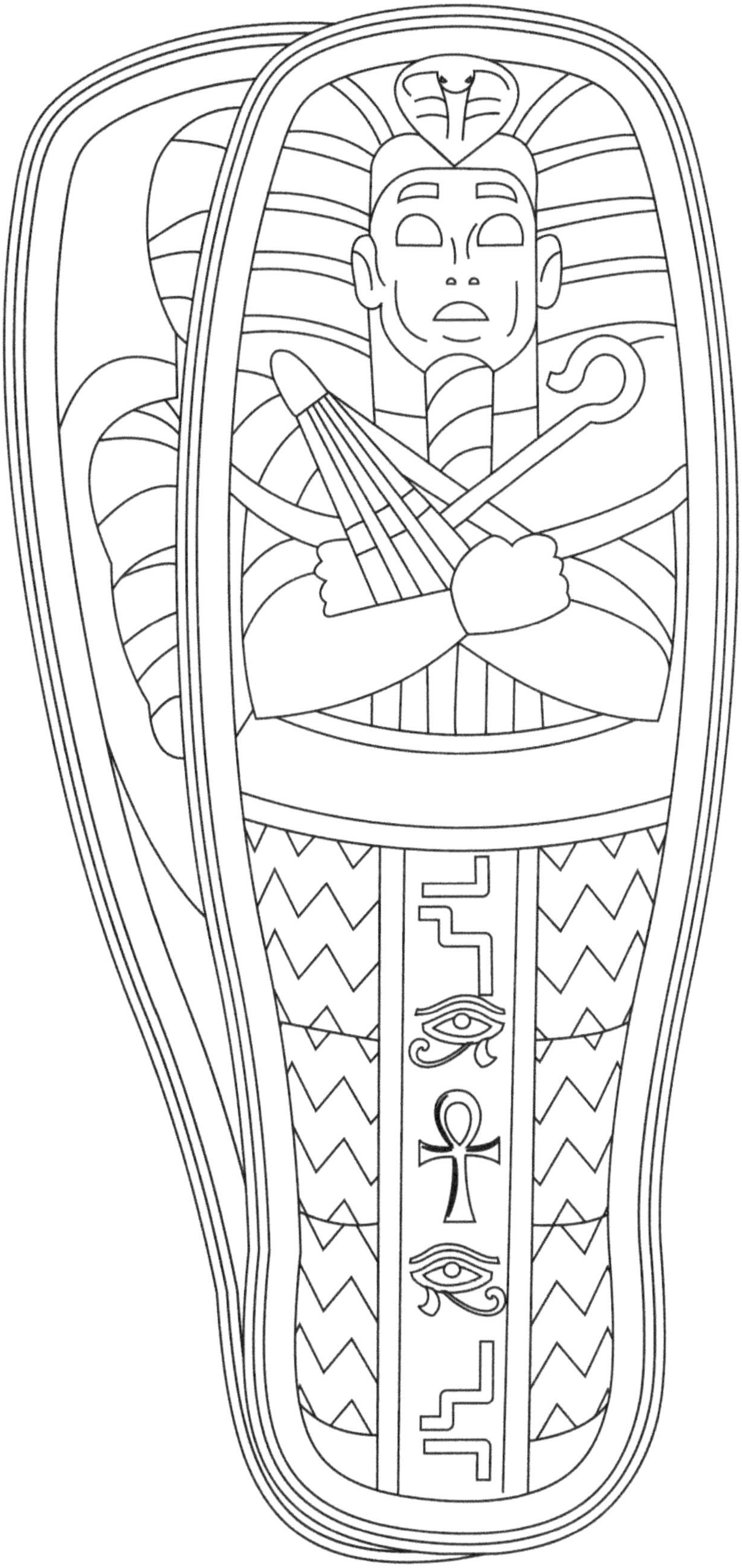

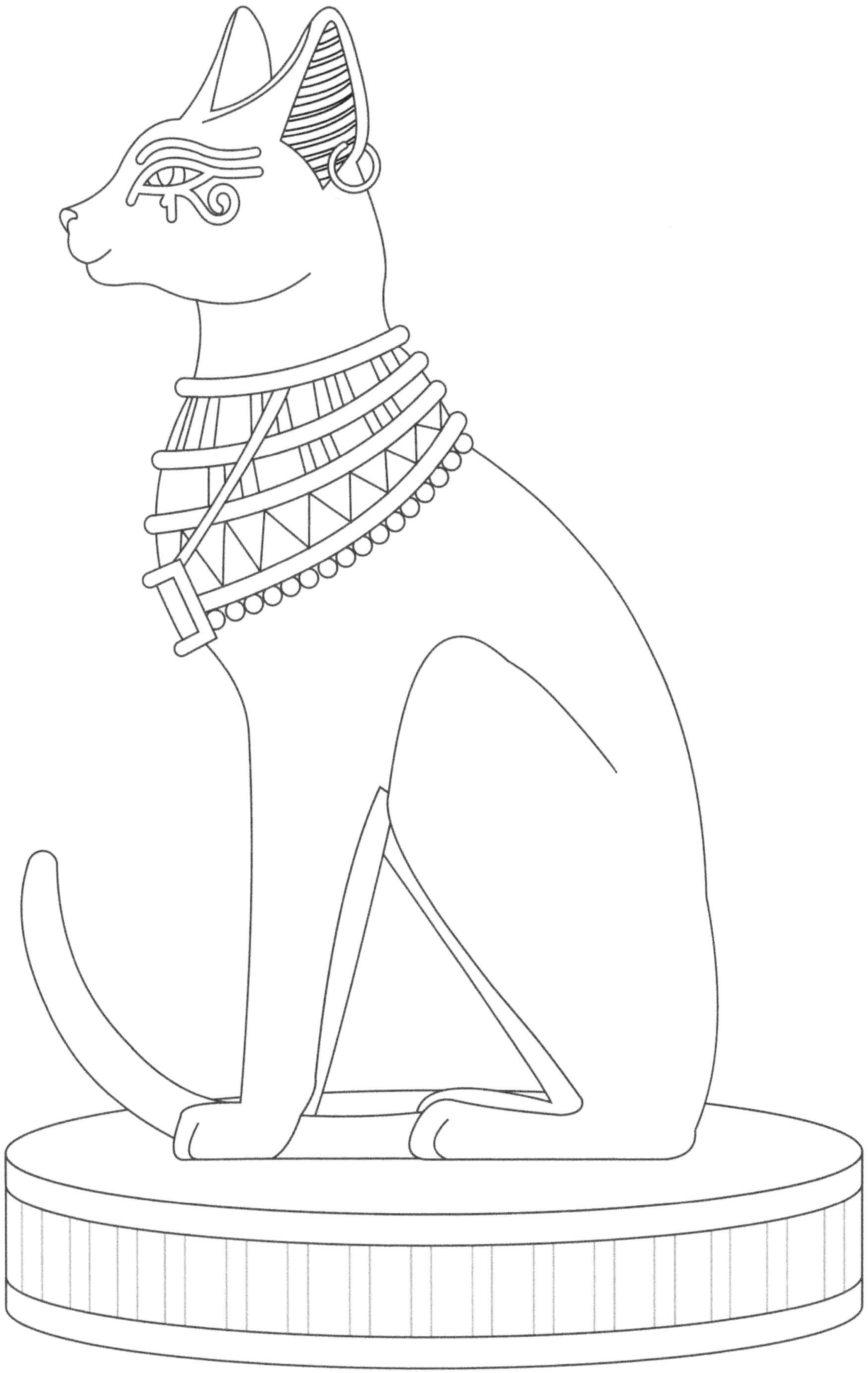

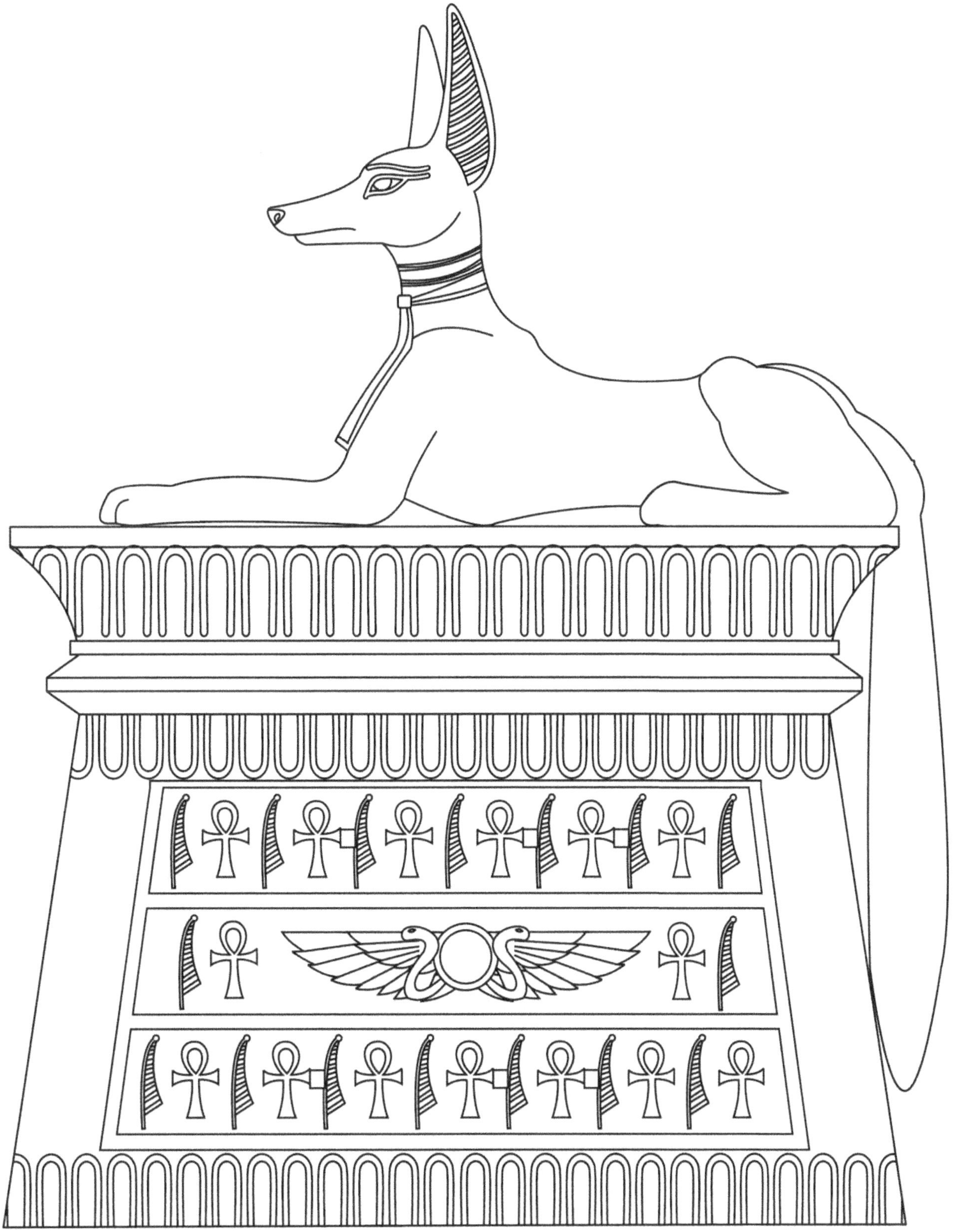

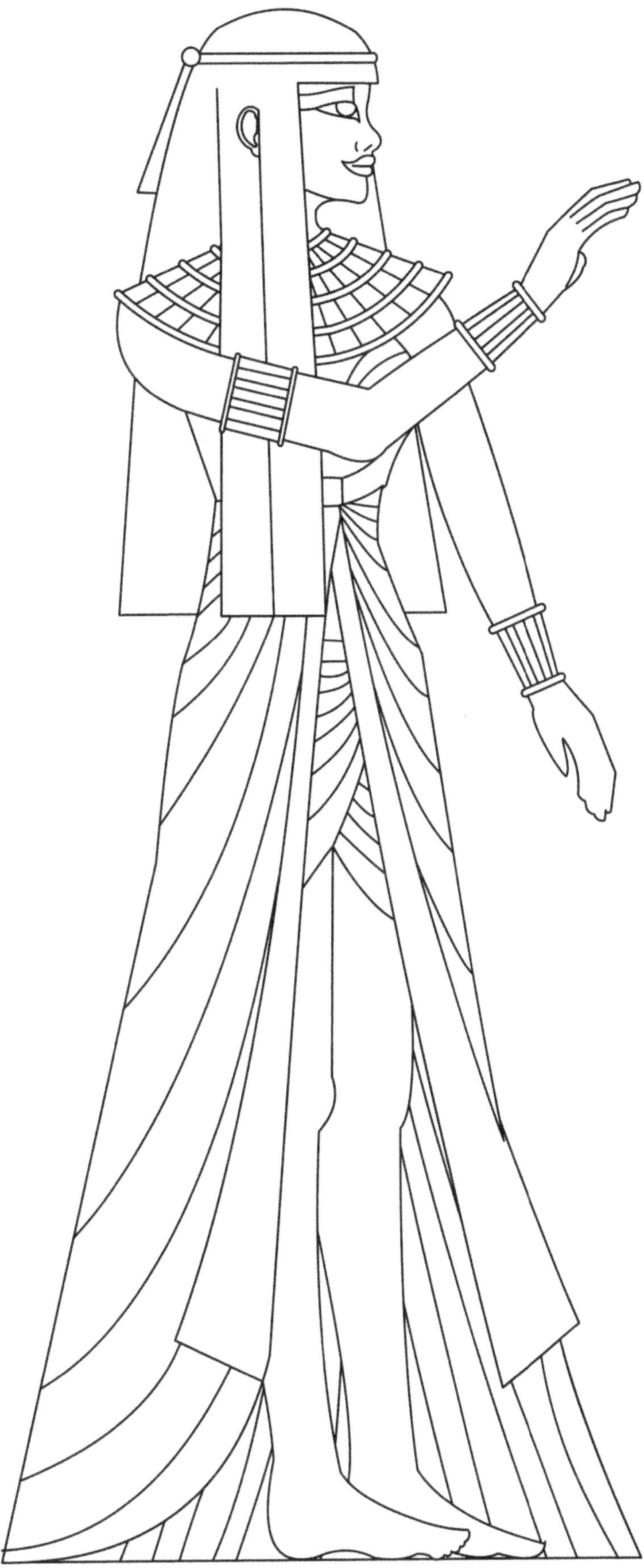

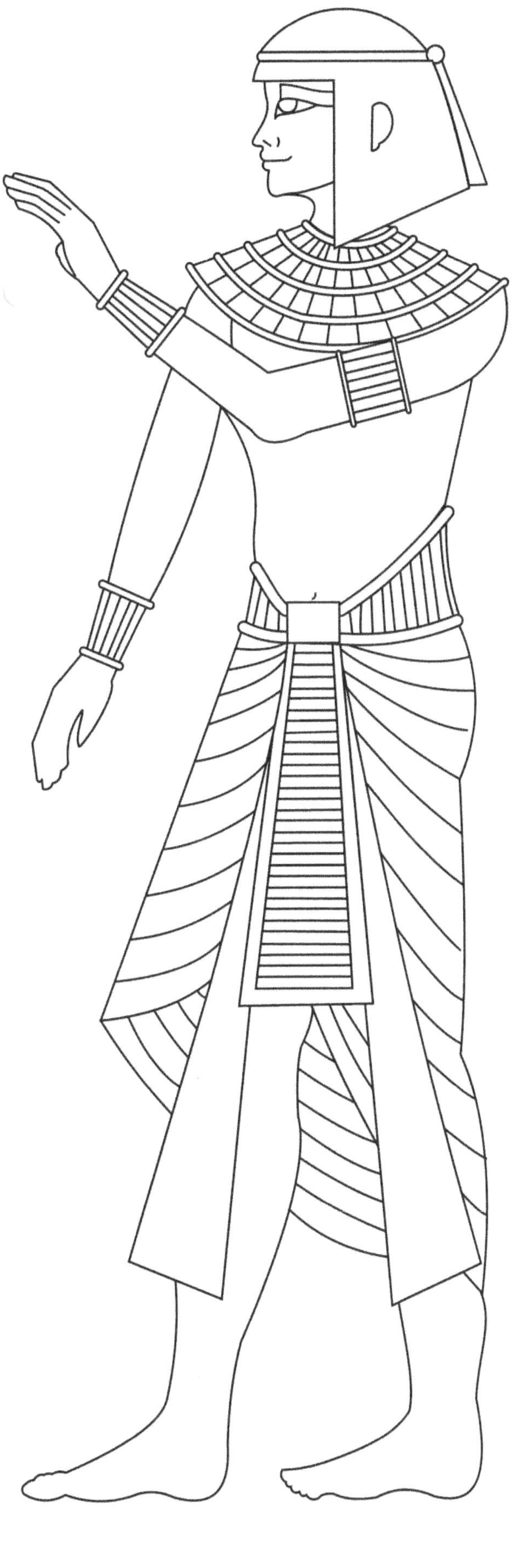

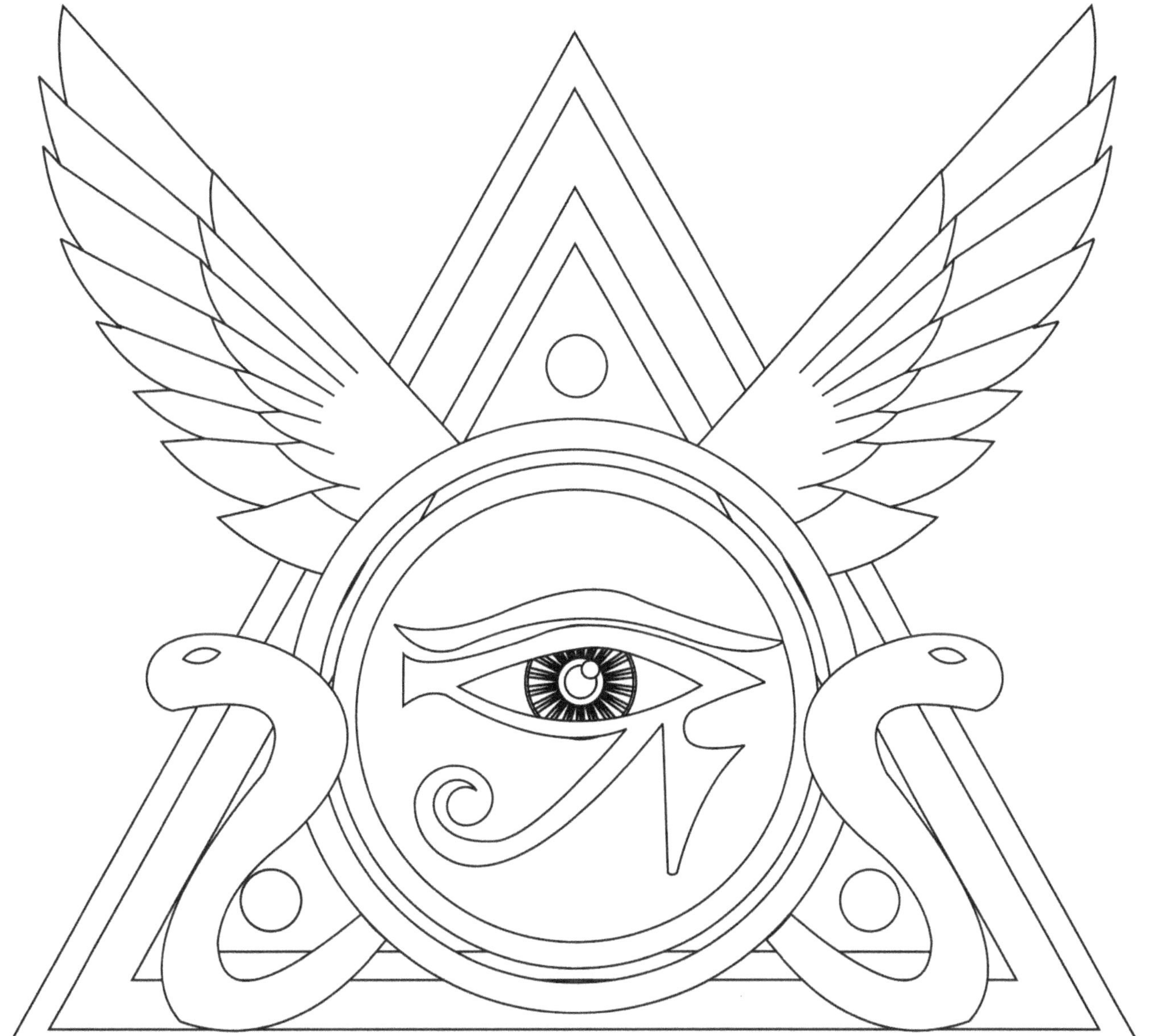

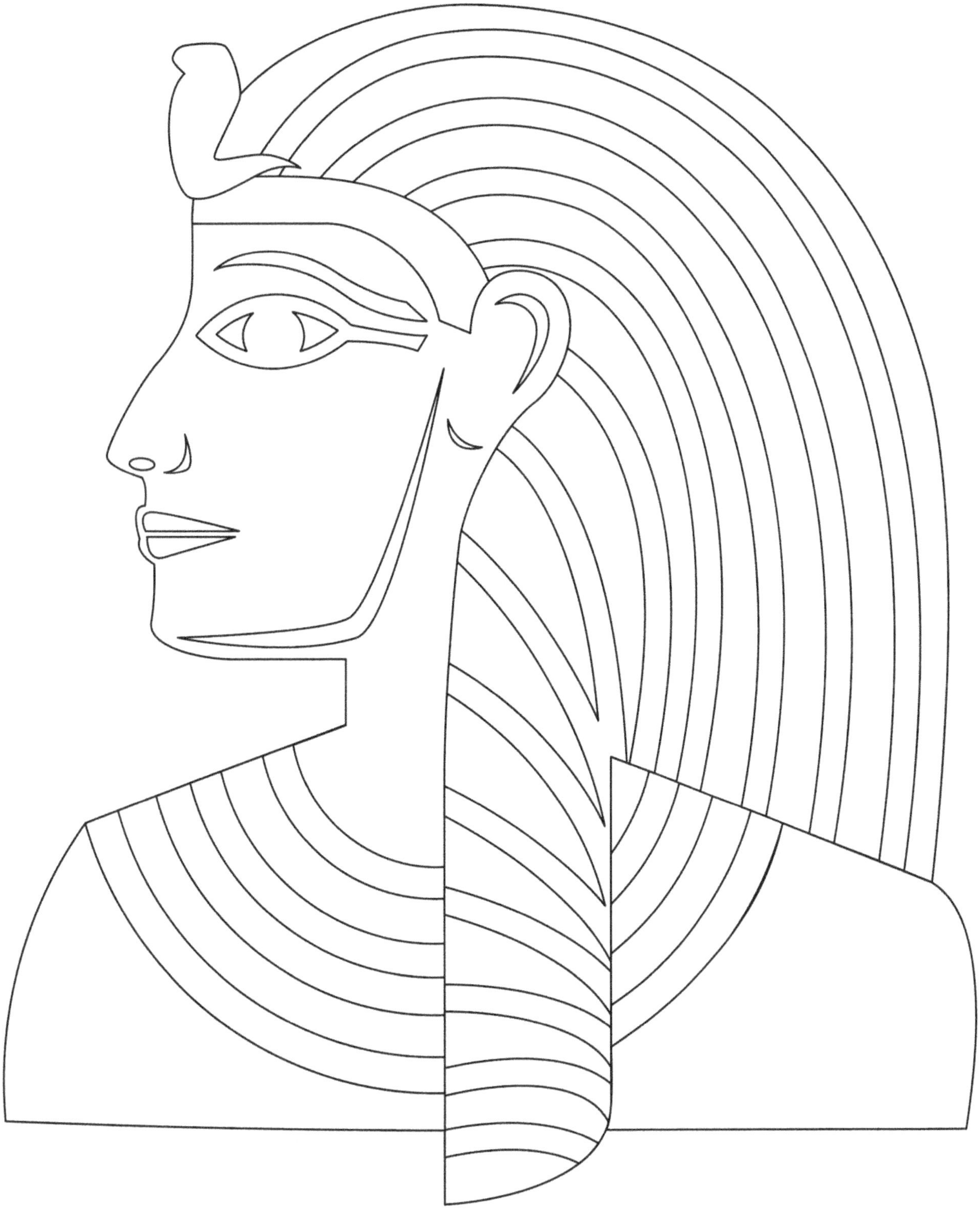

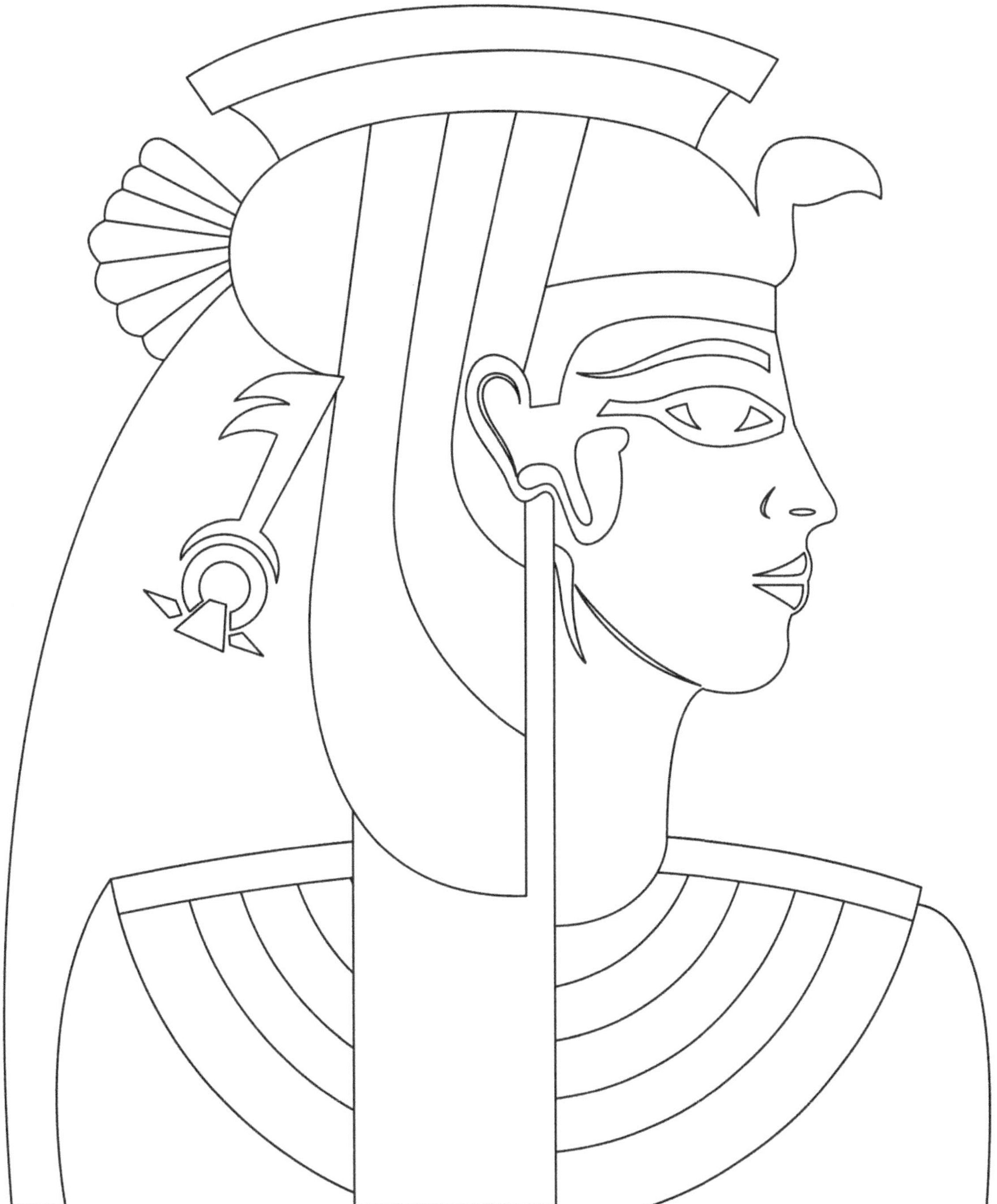

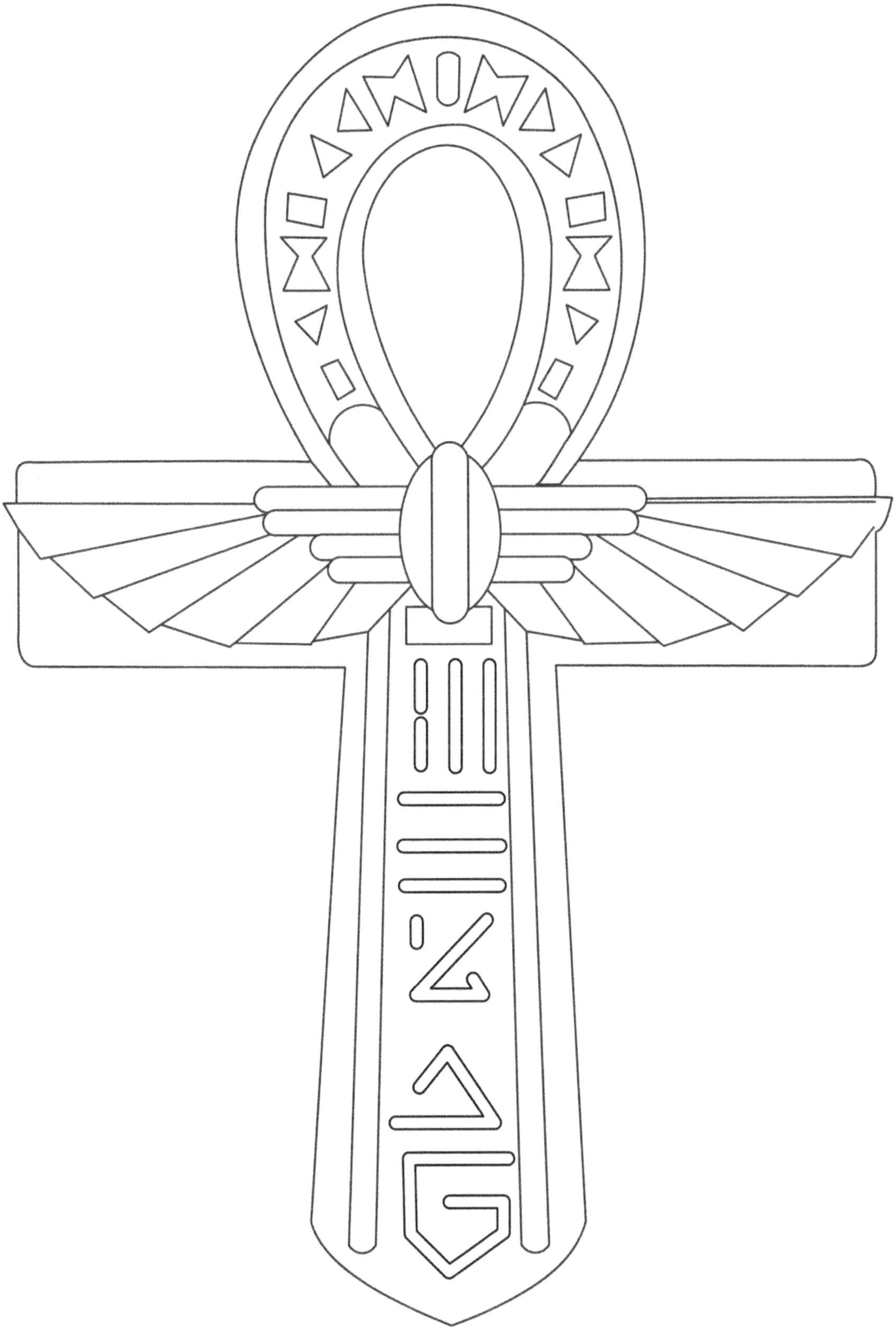

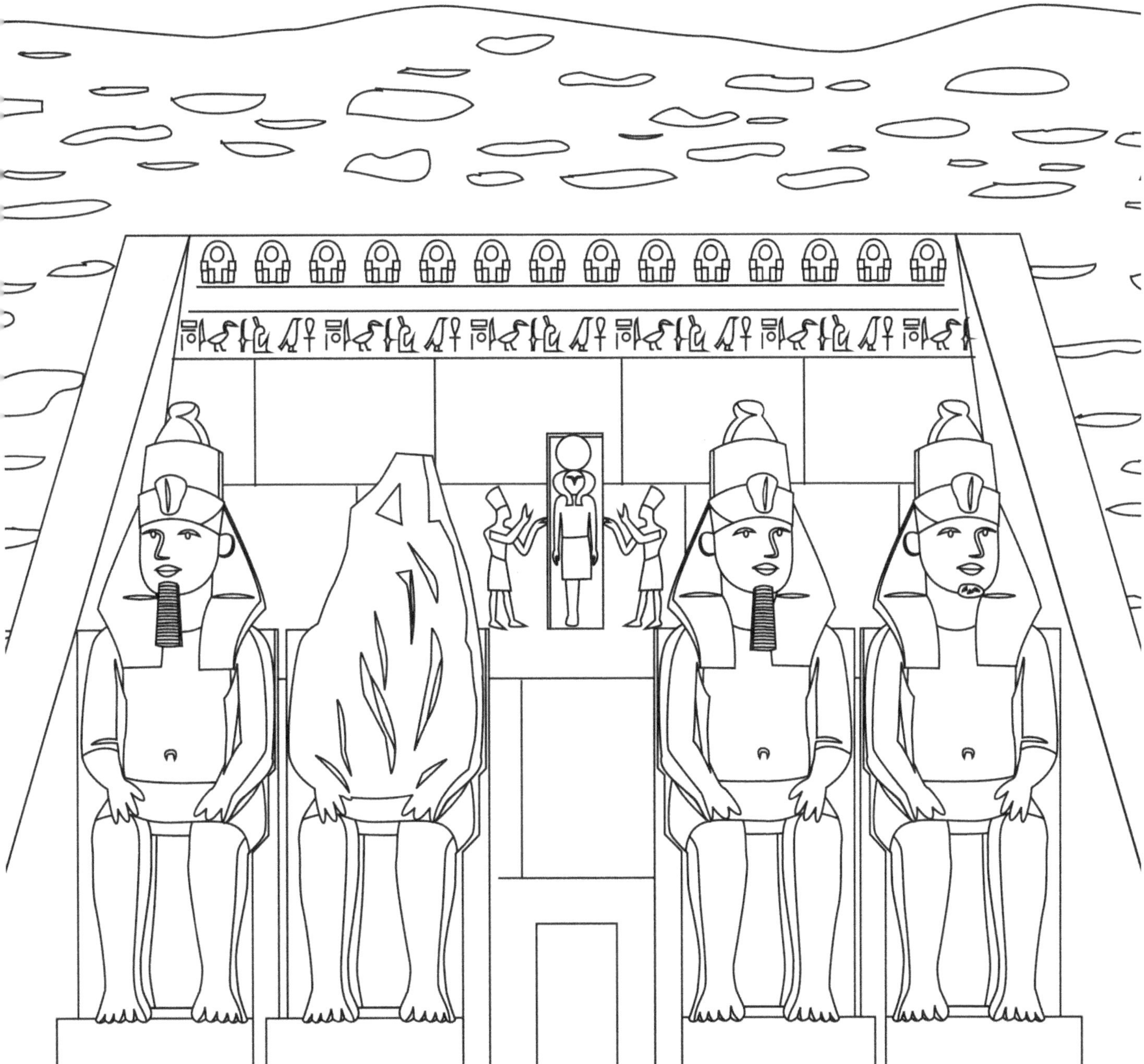

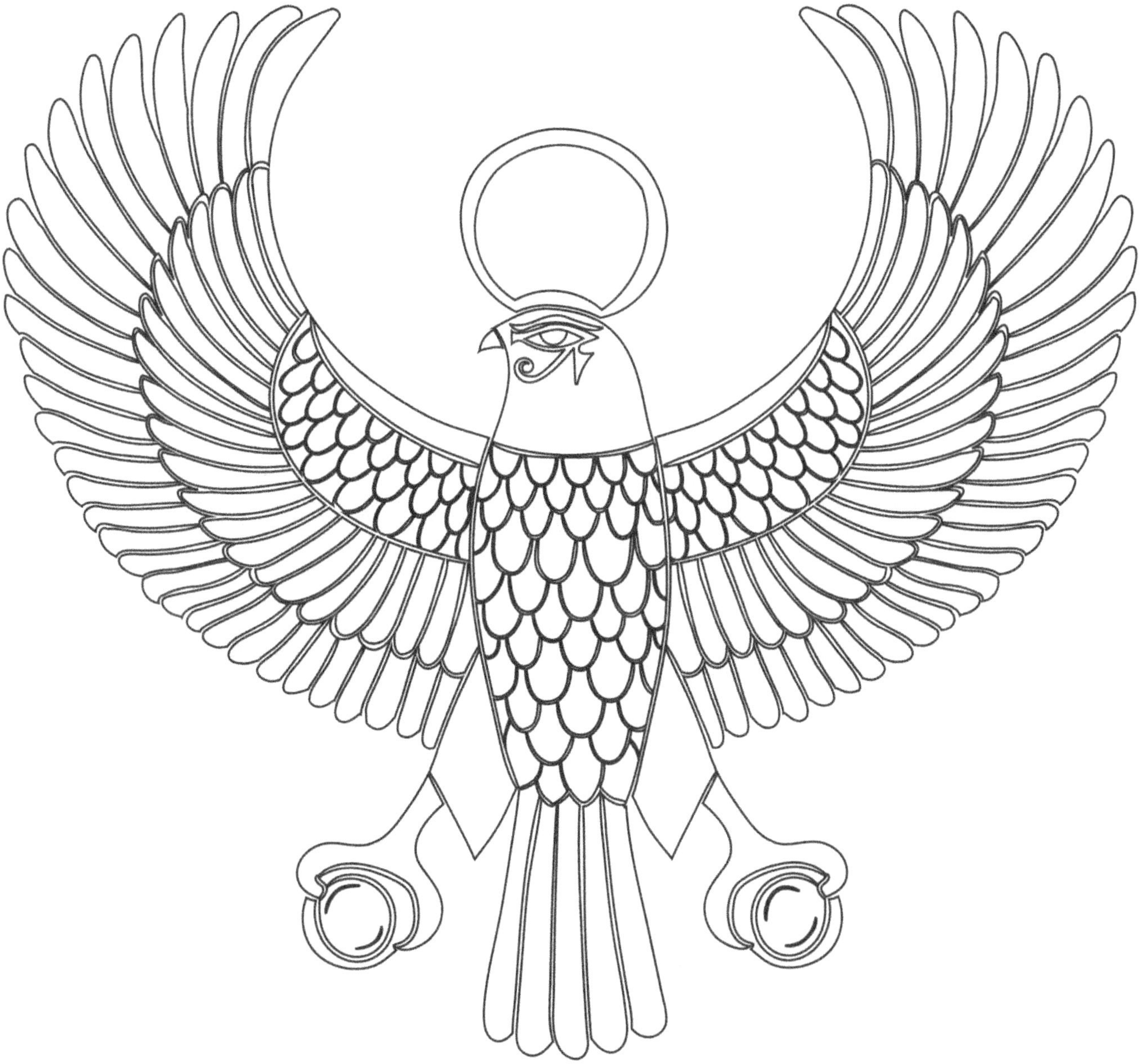

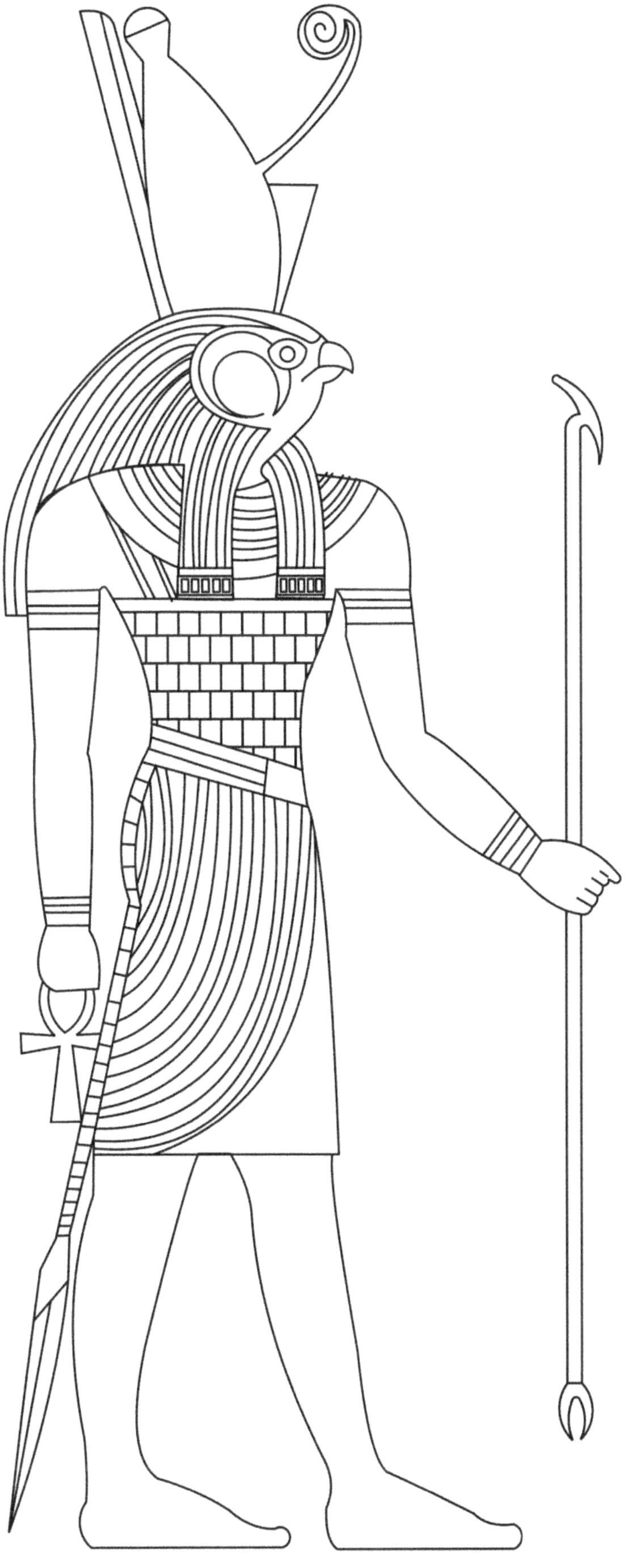

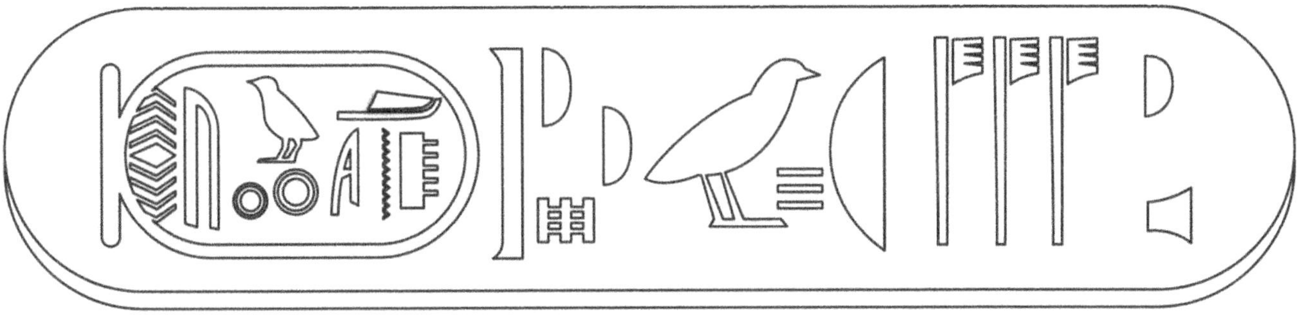

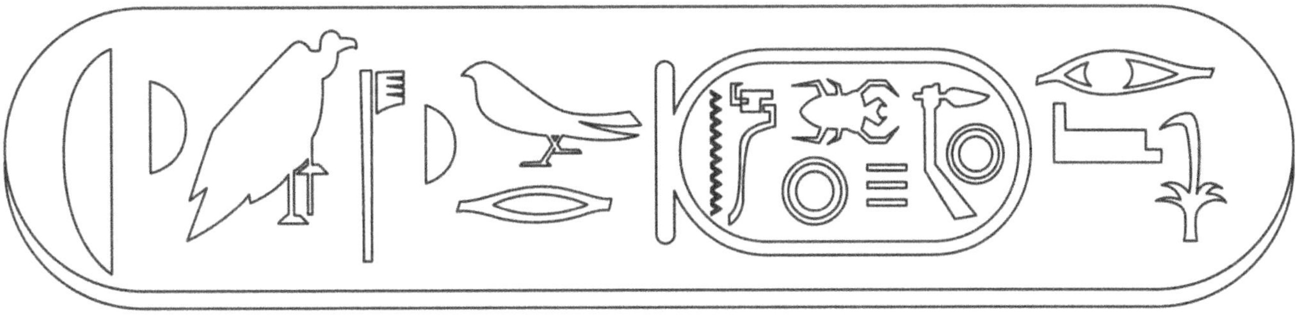

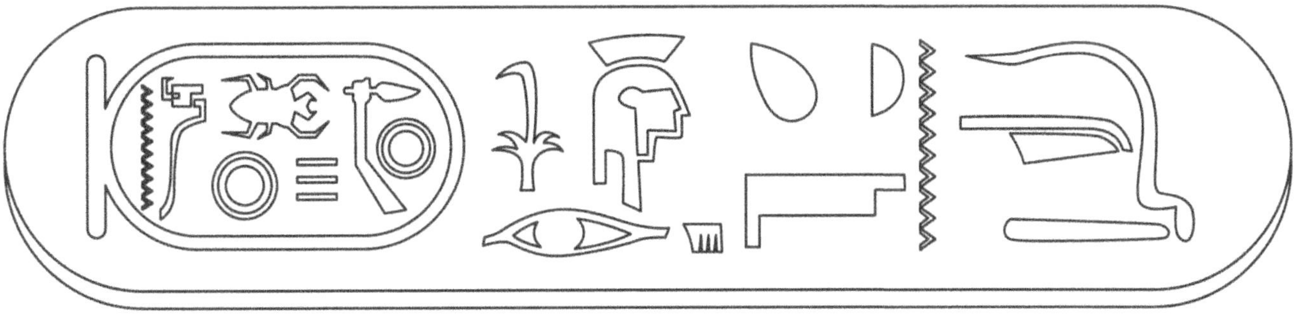

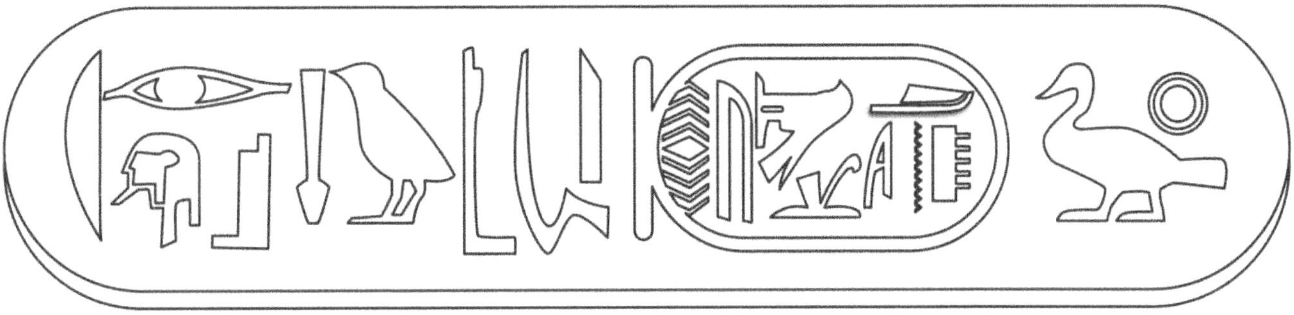

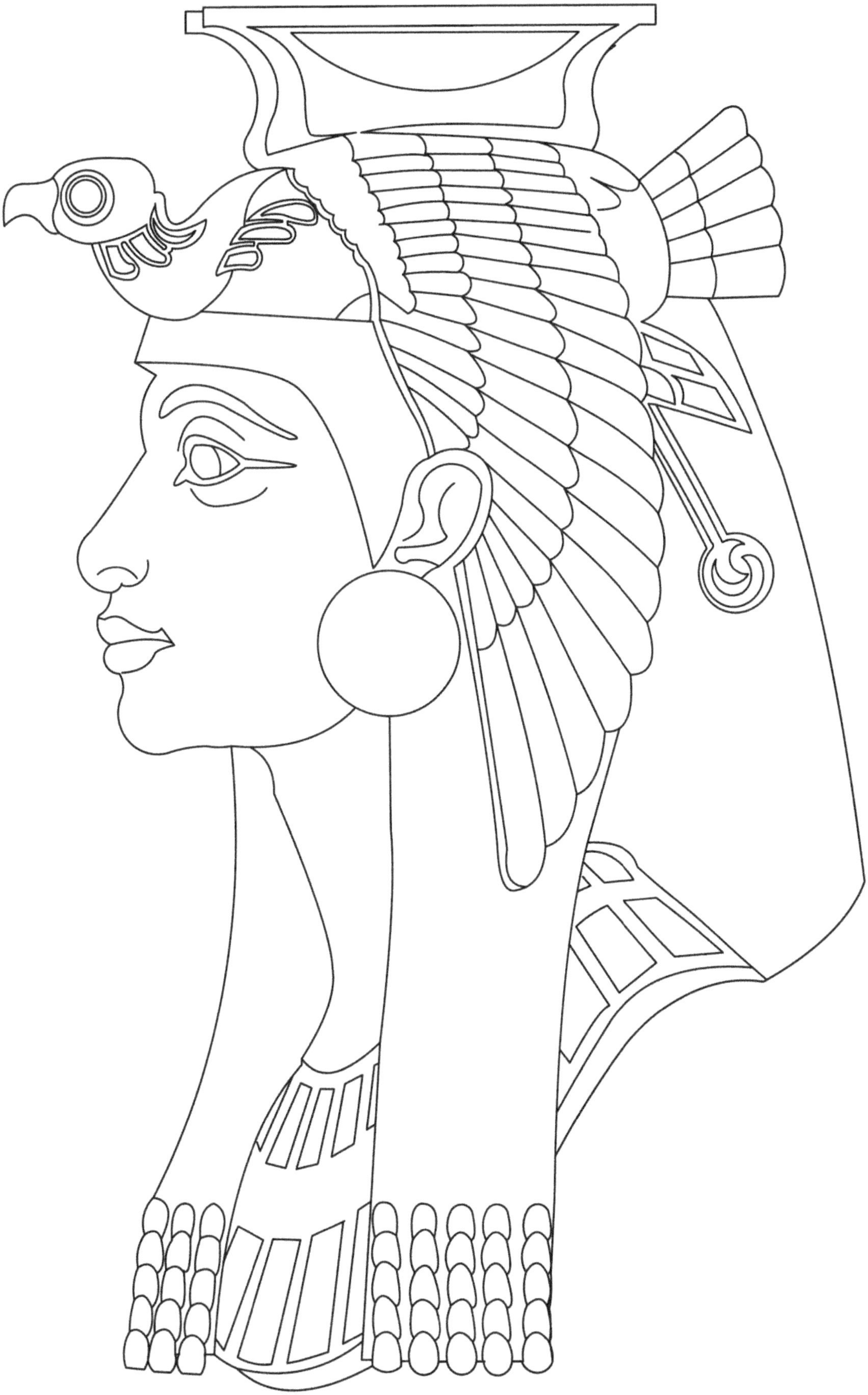

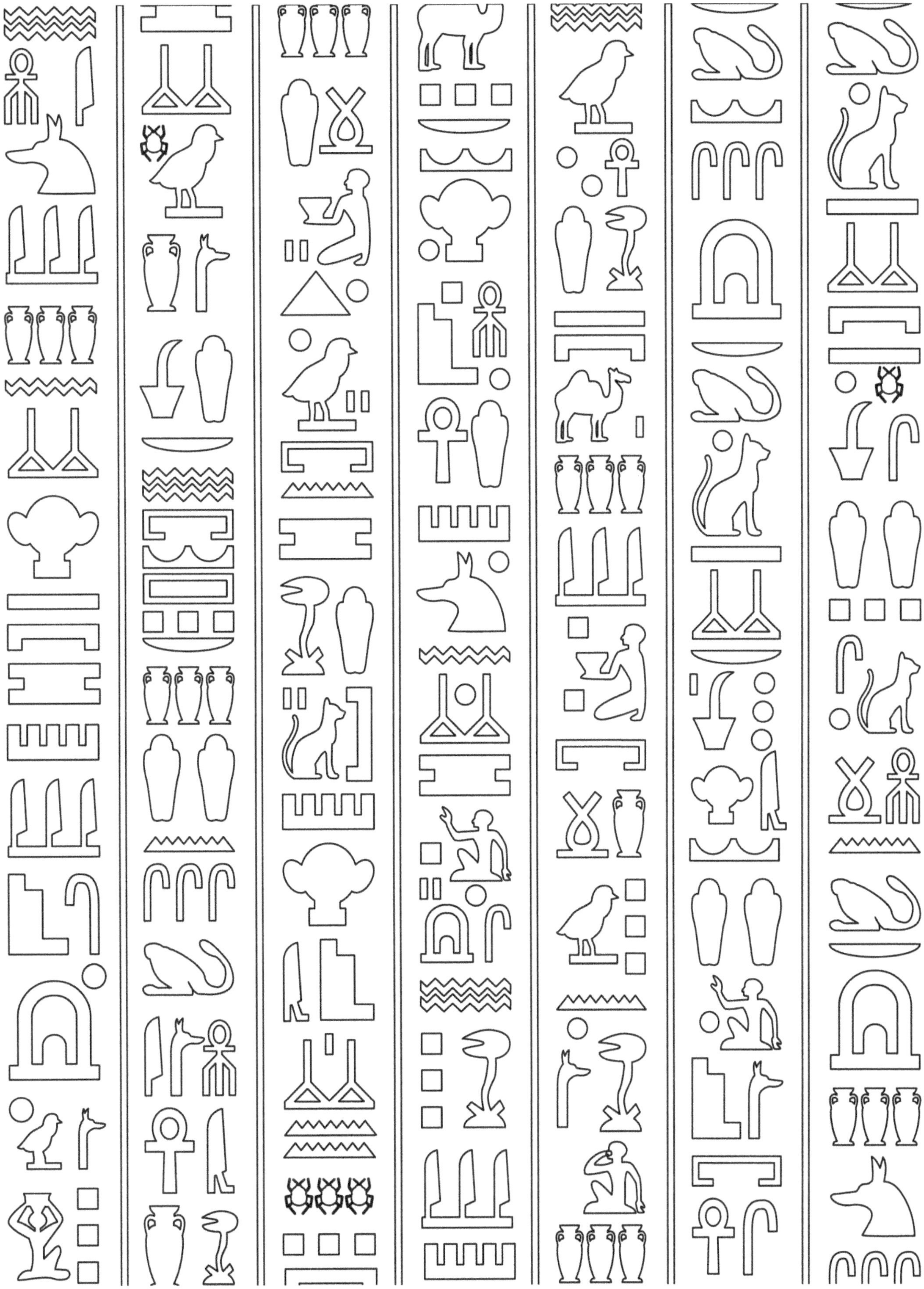

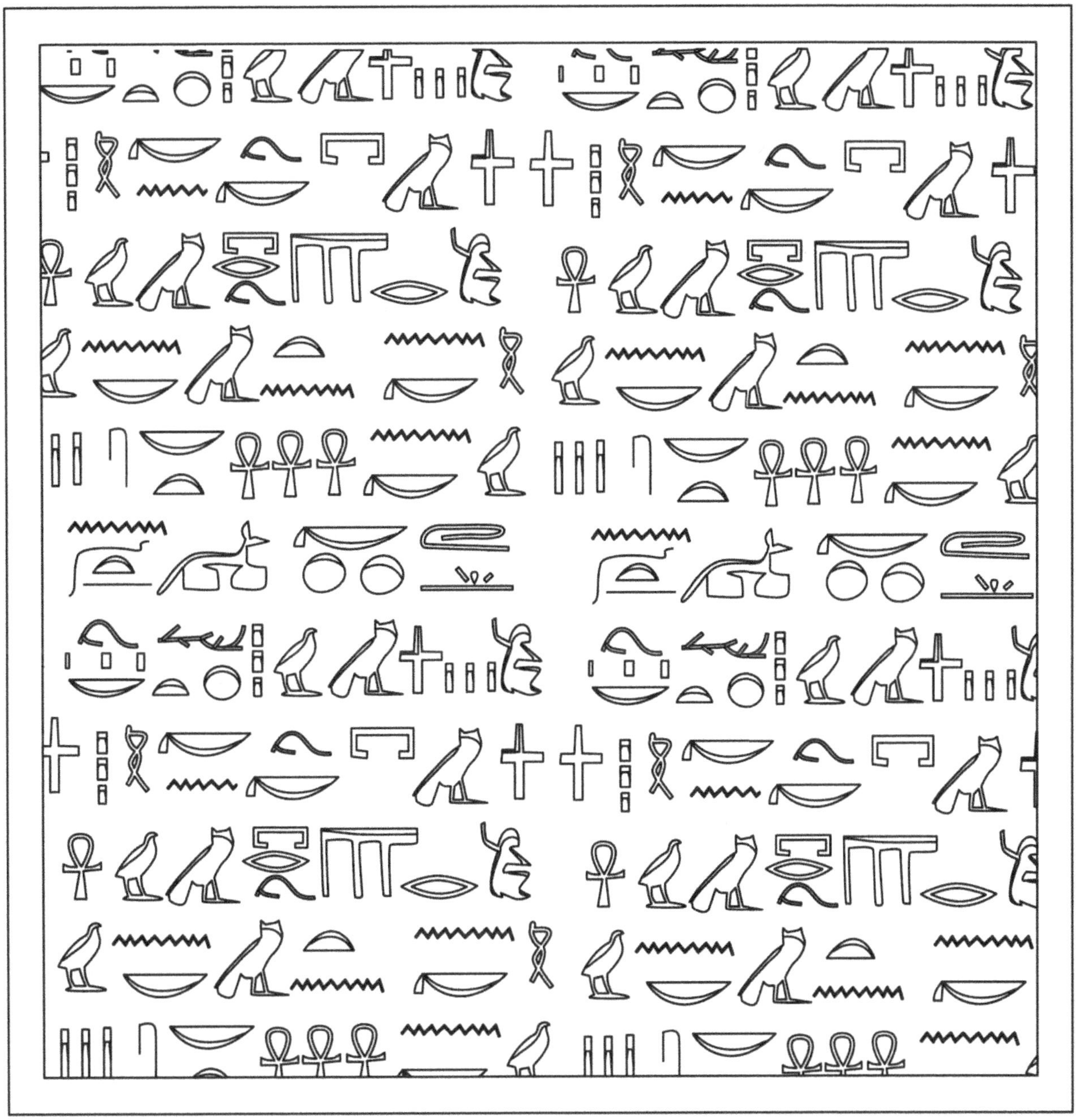

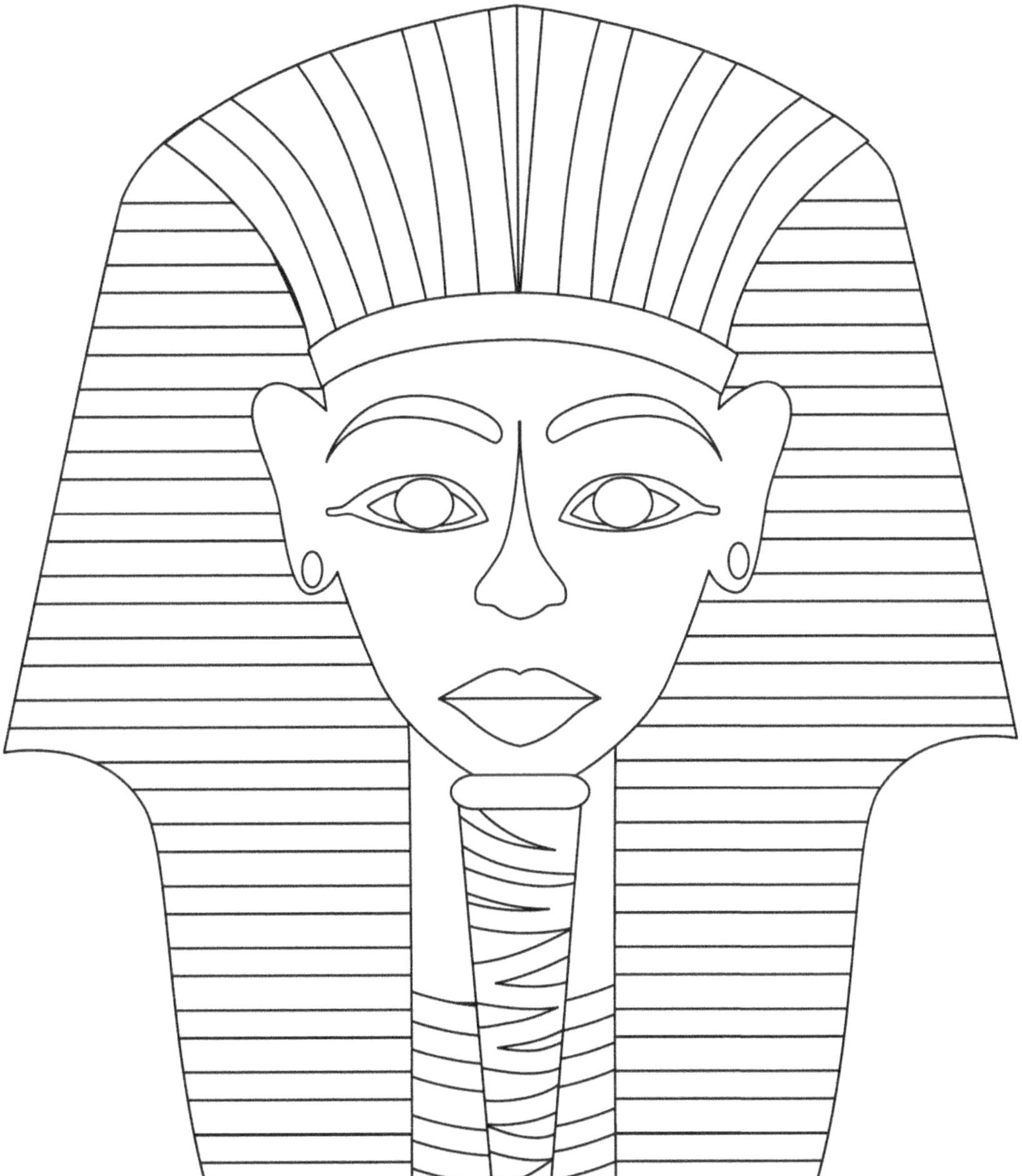

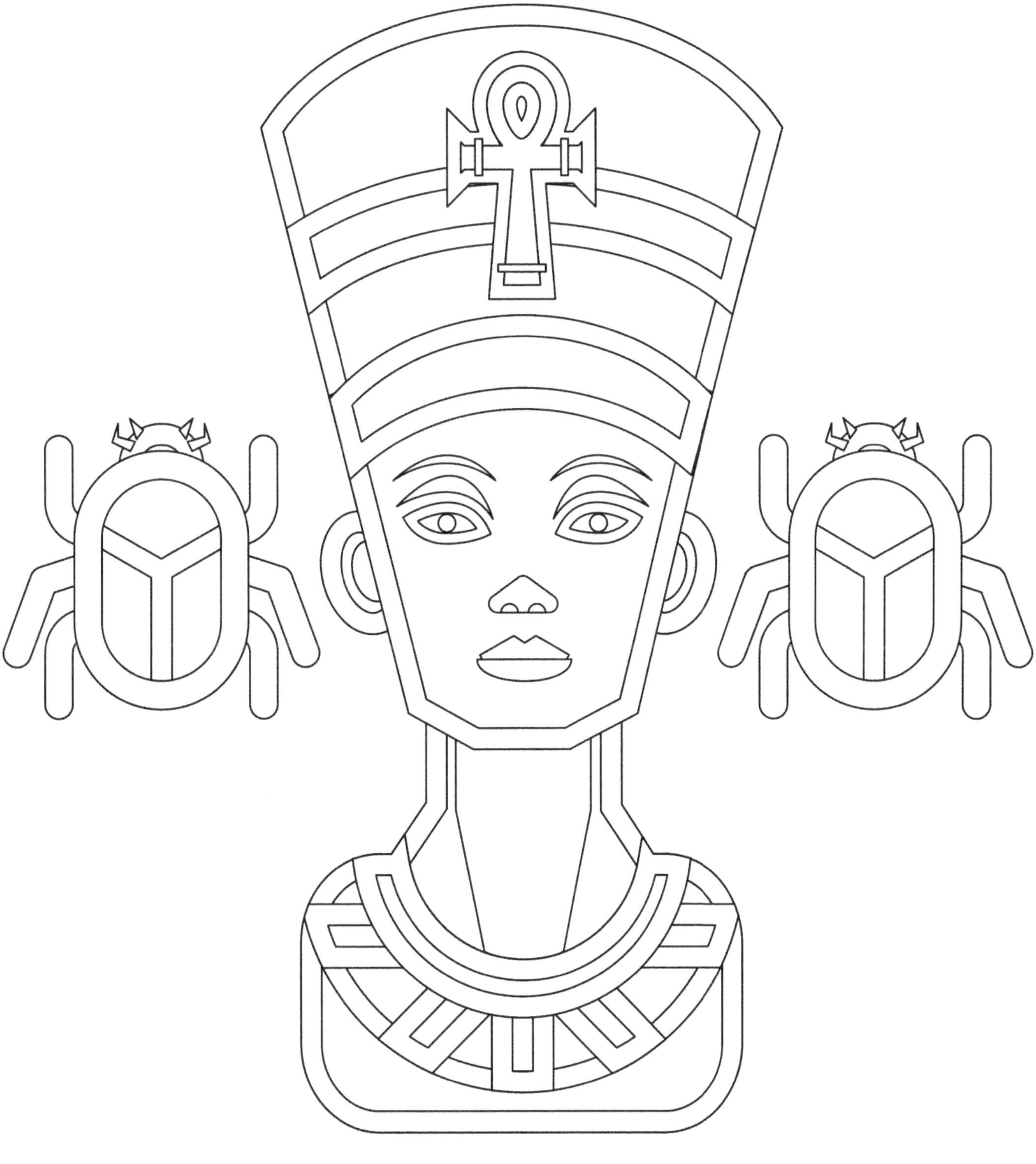

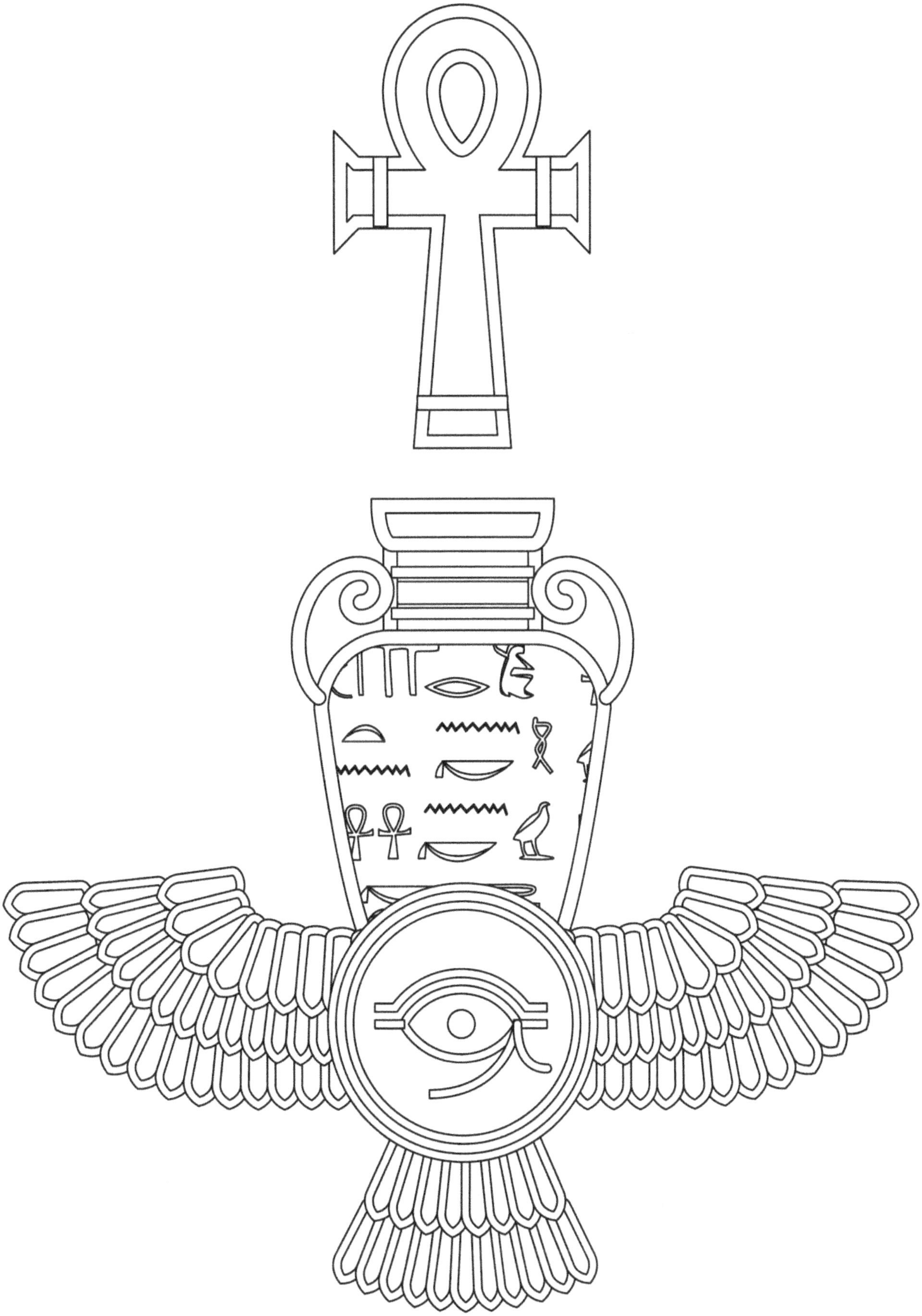

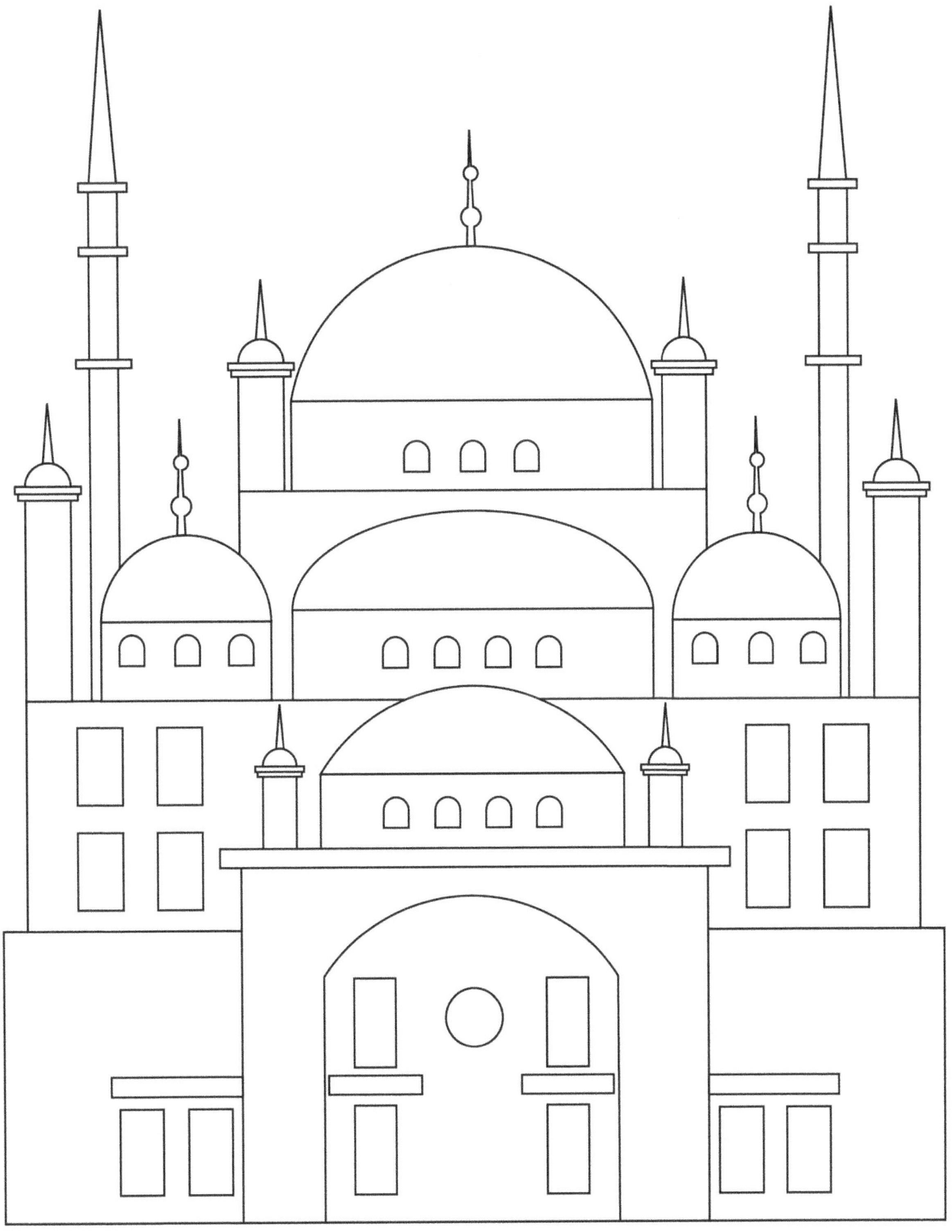

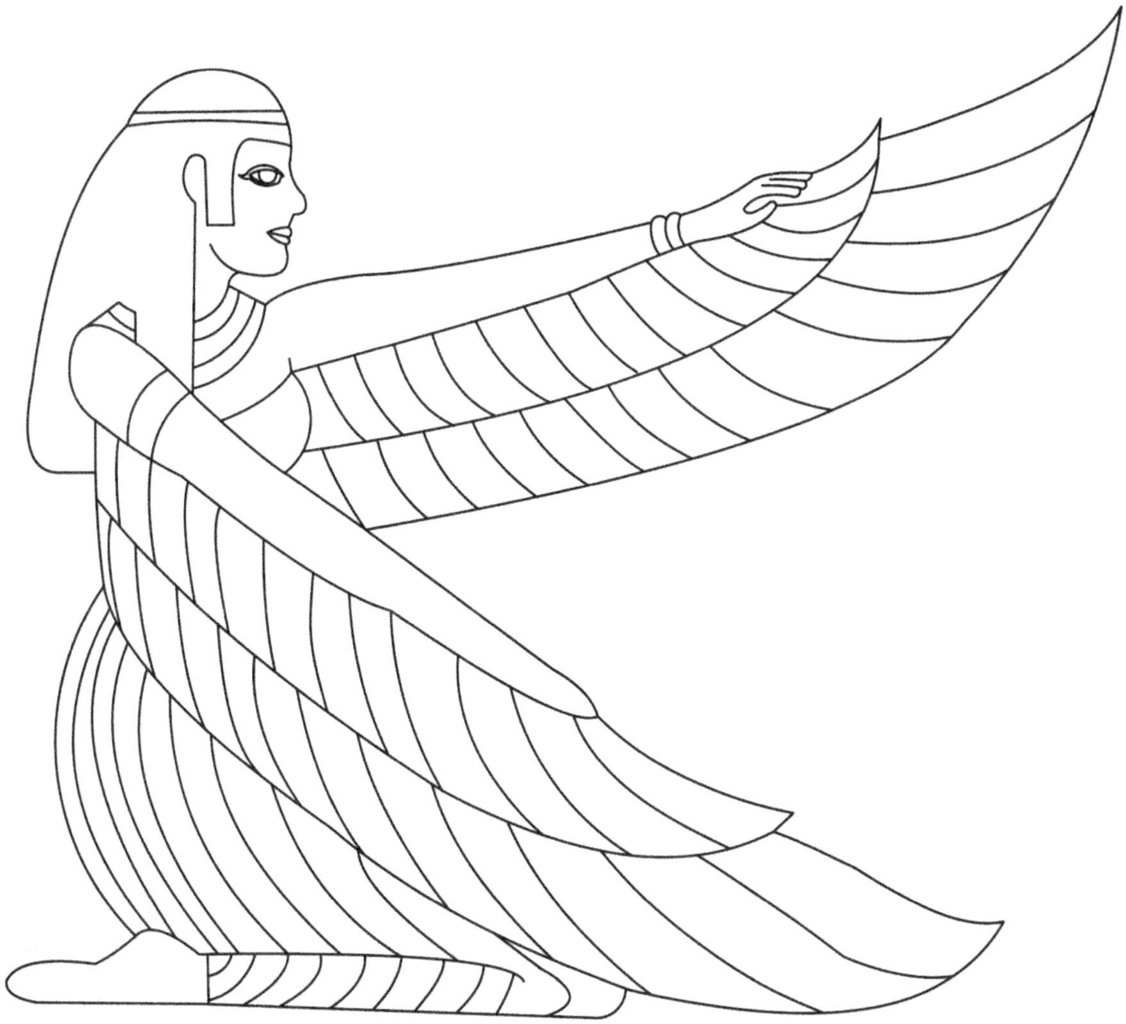

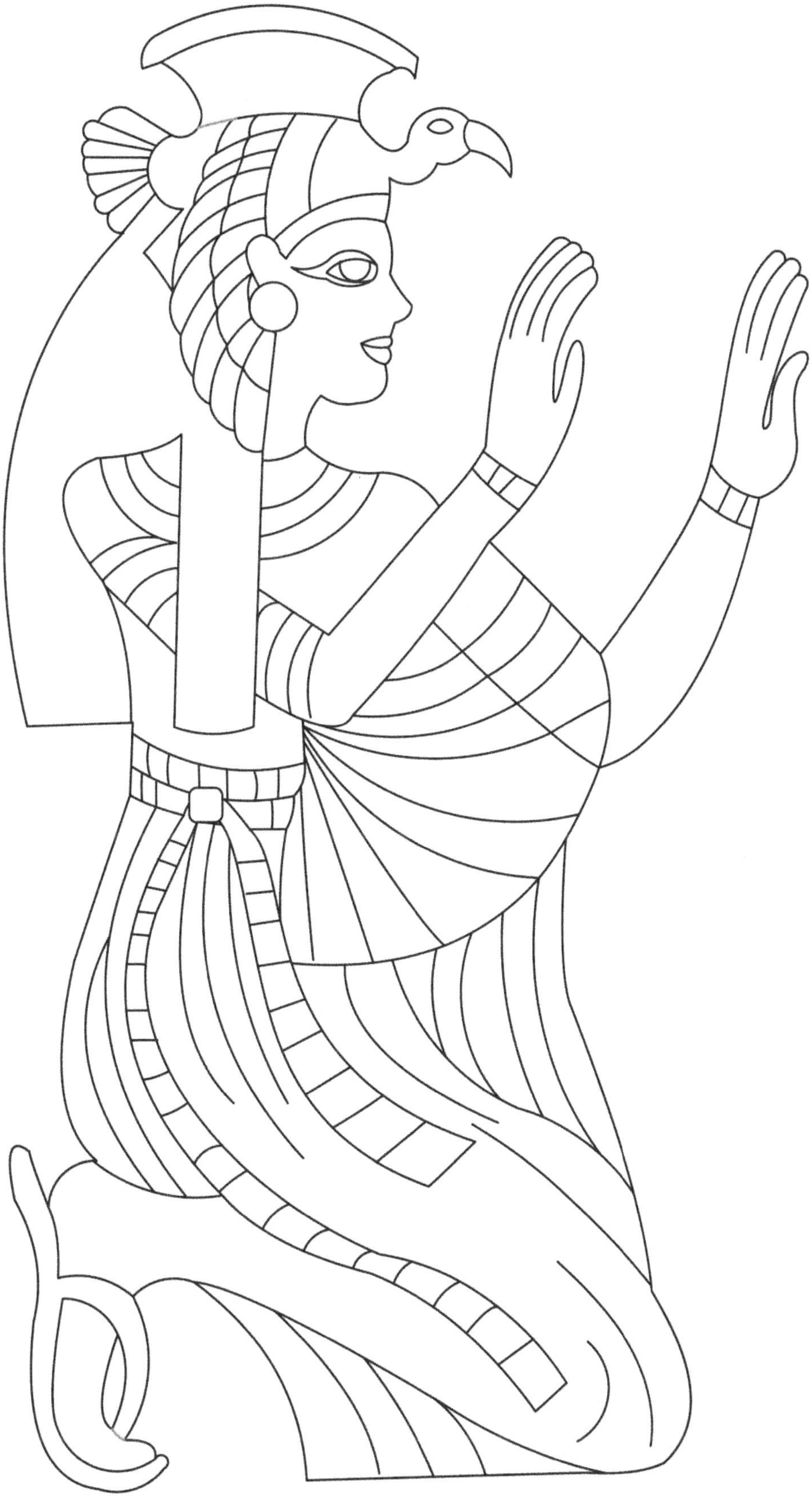

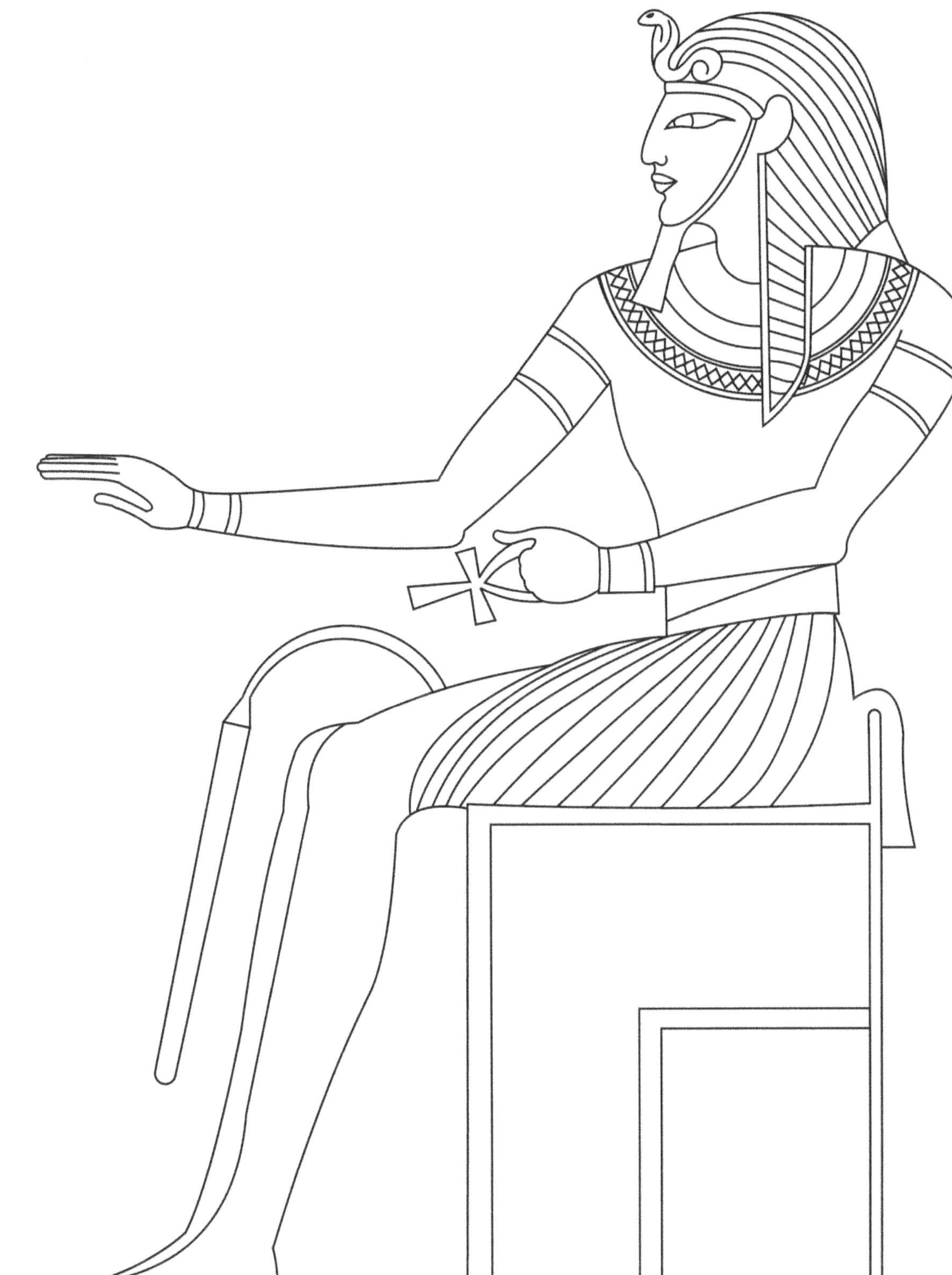

Bonus

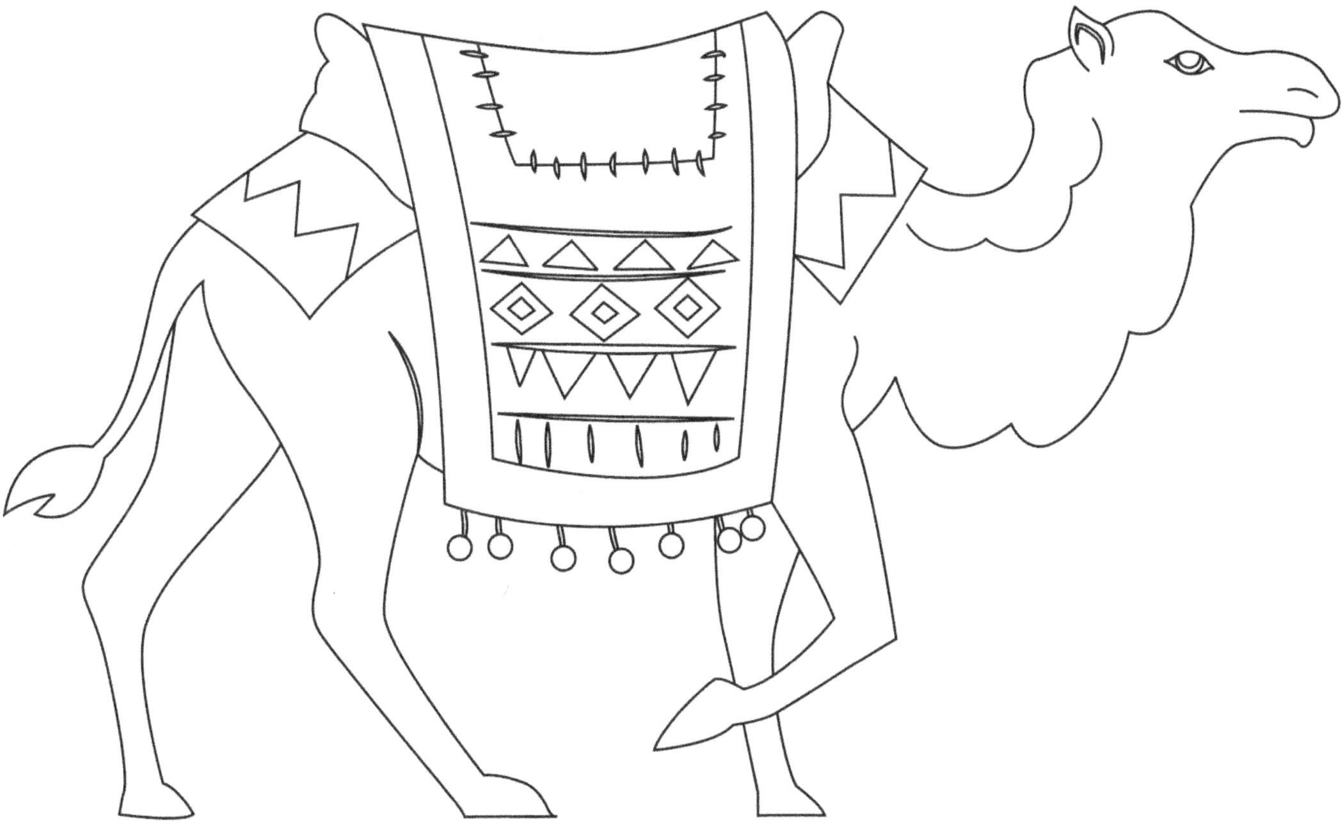

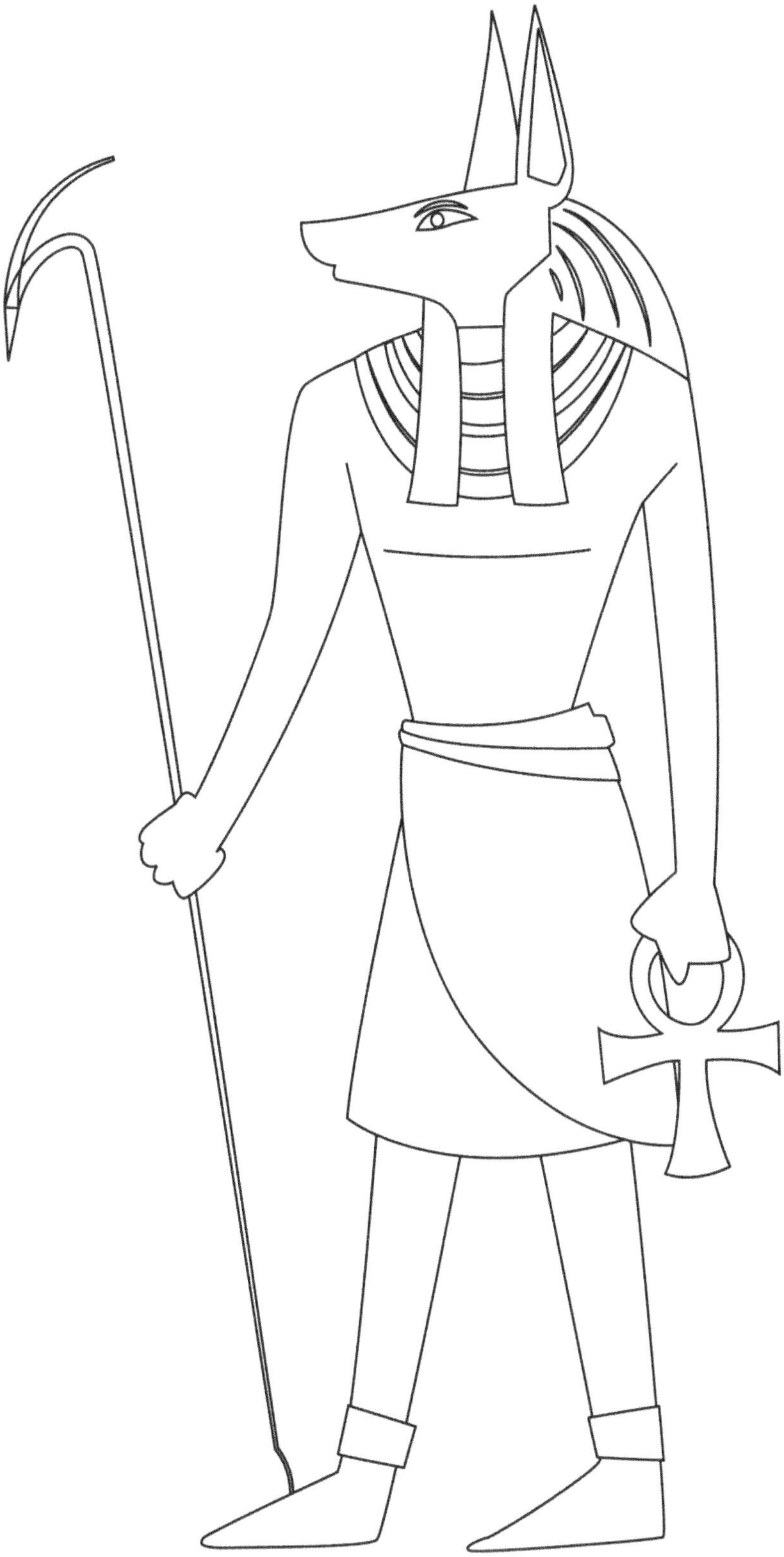

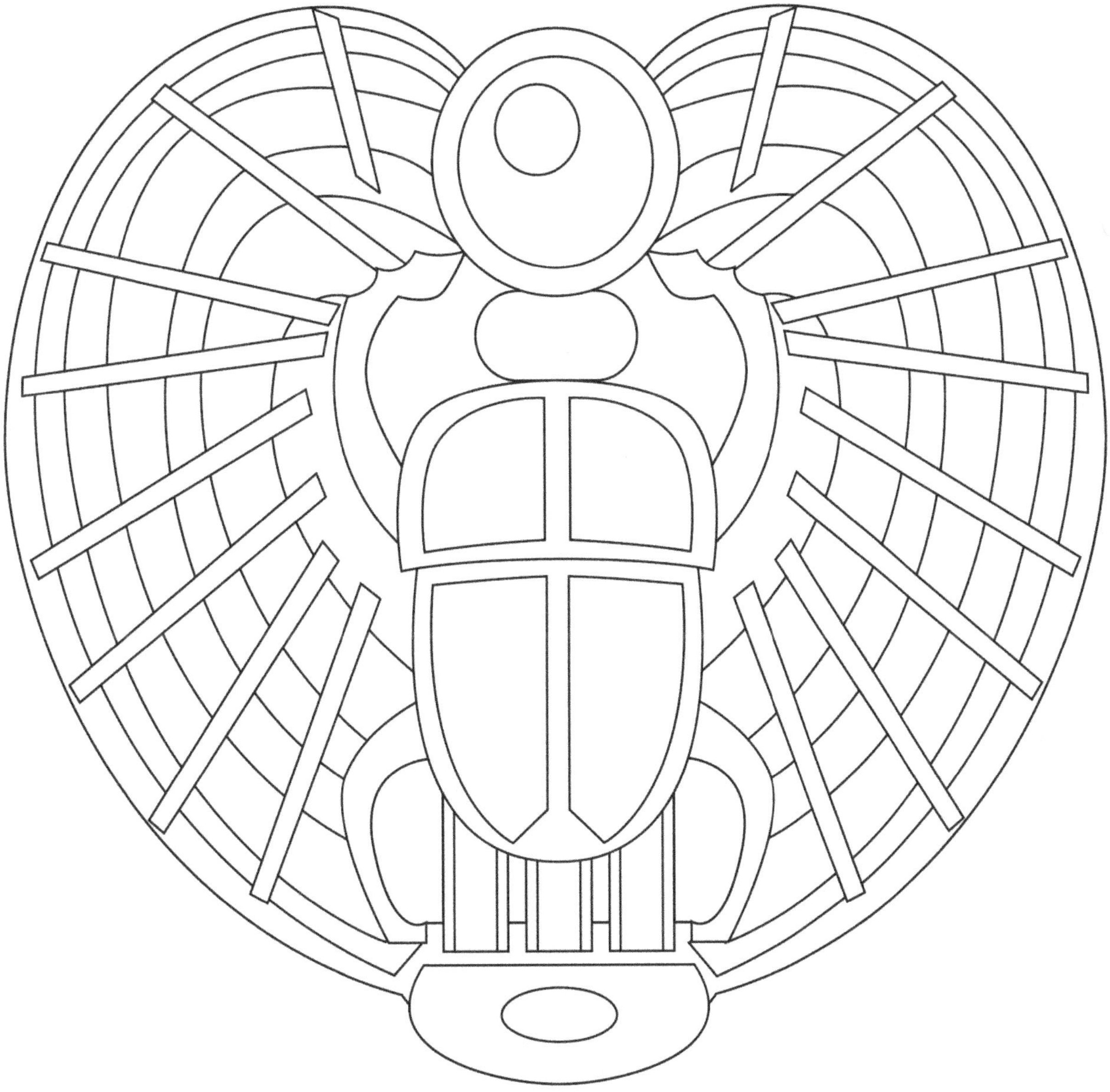

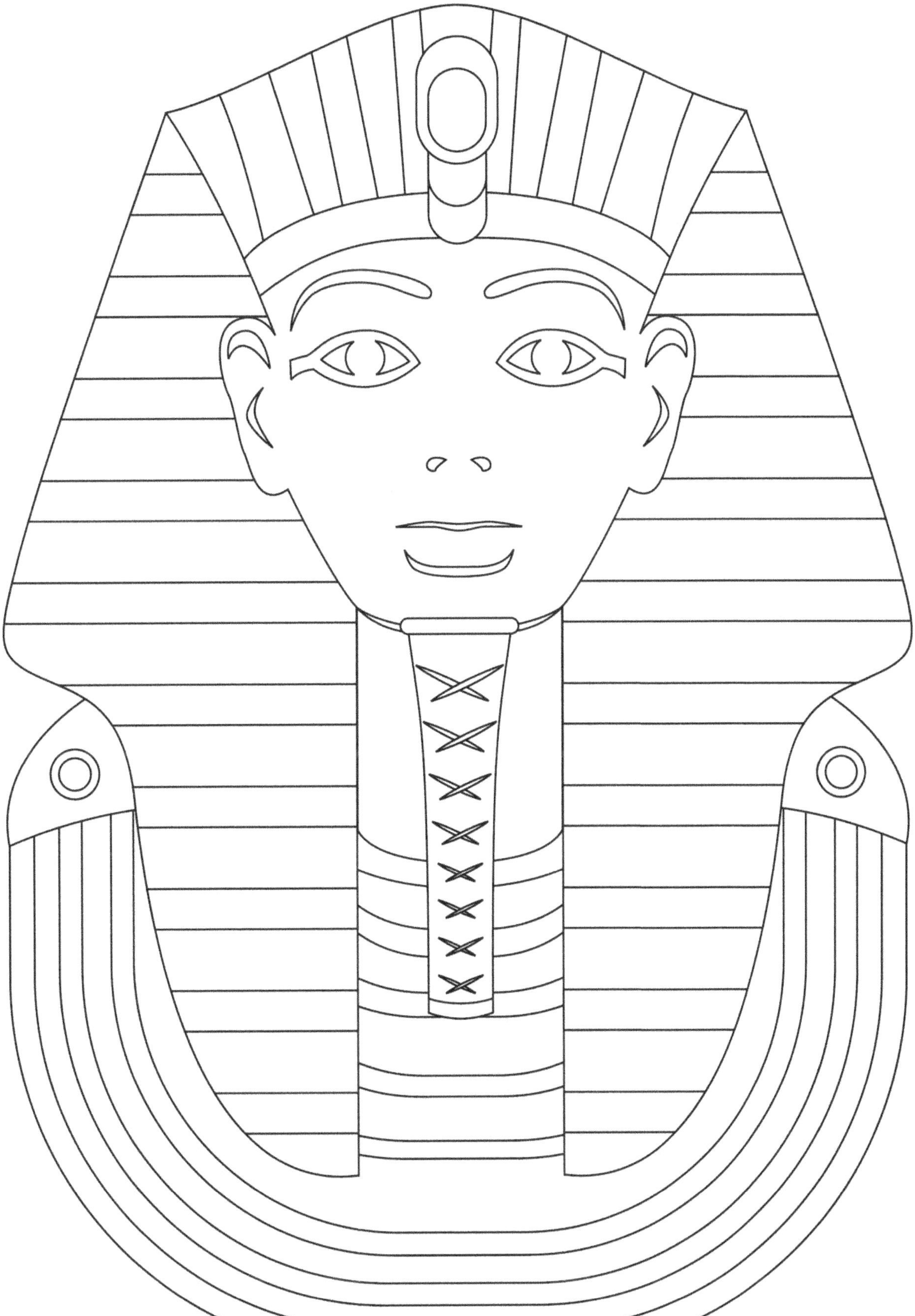

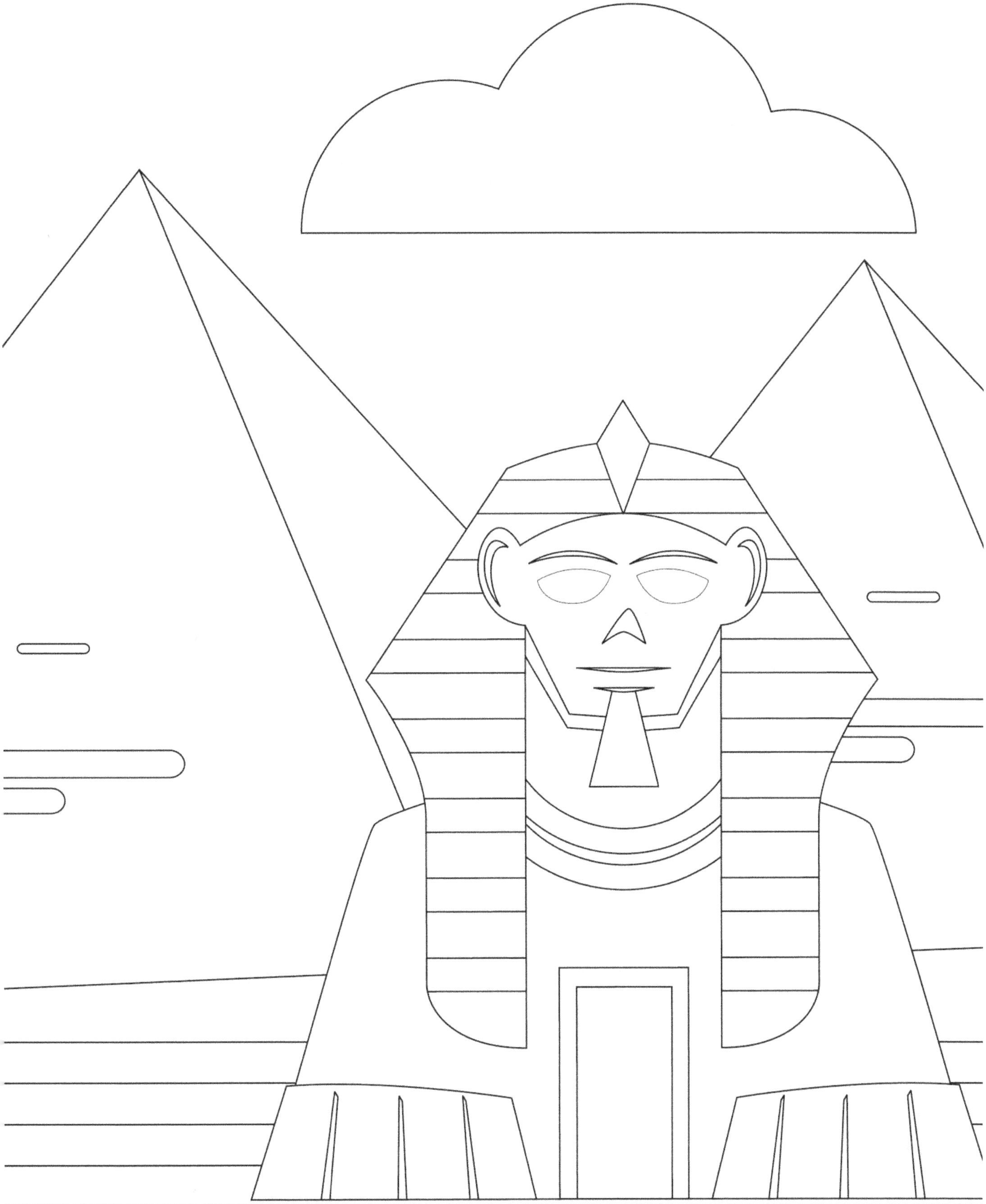

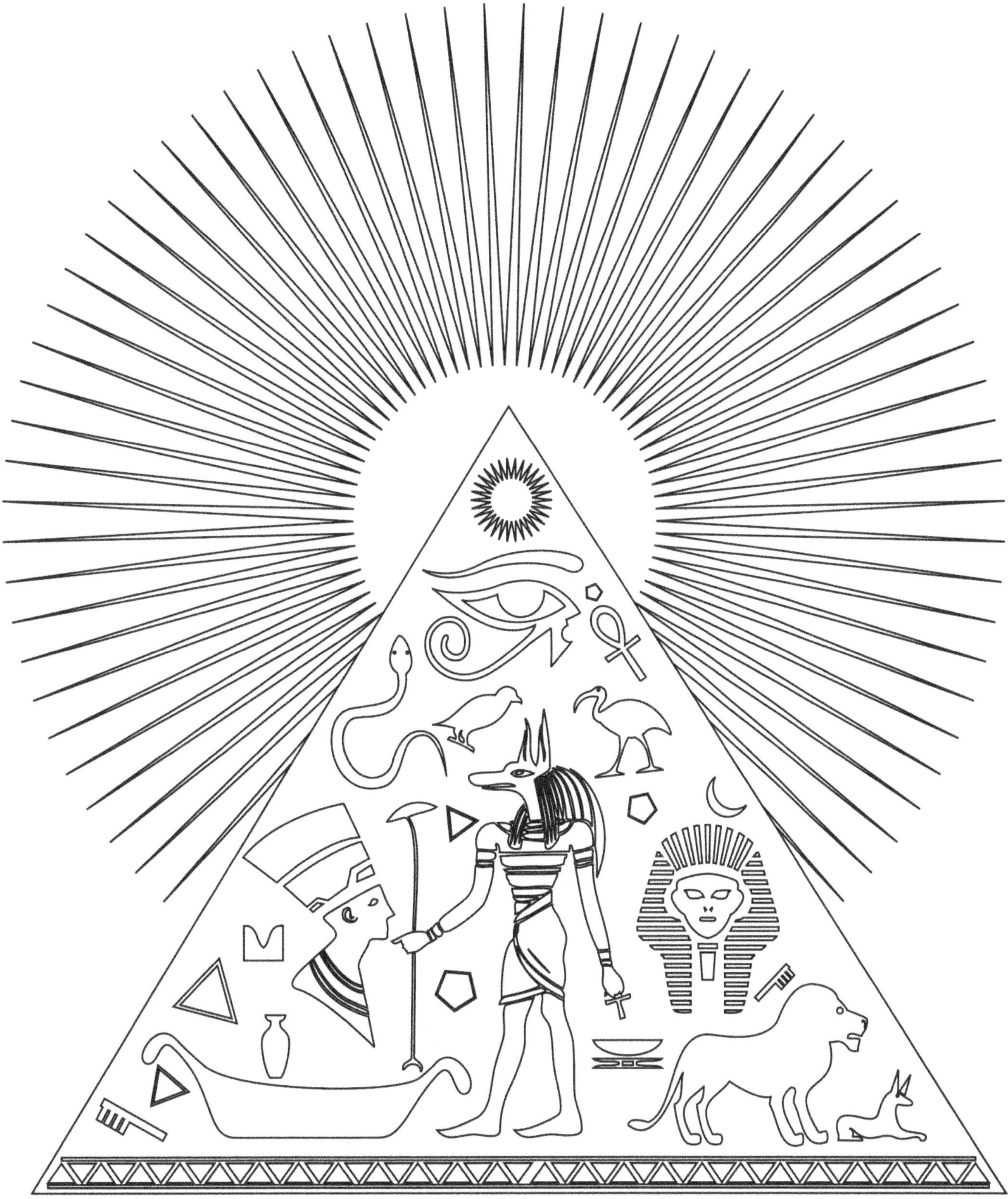

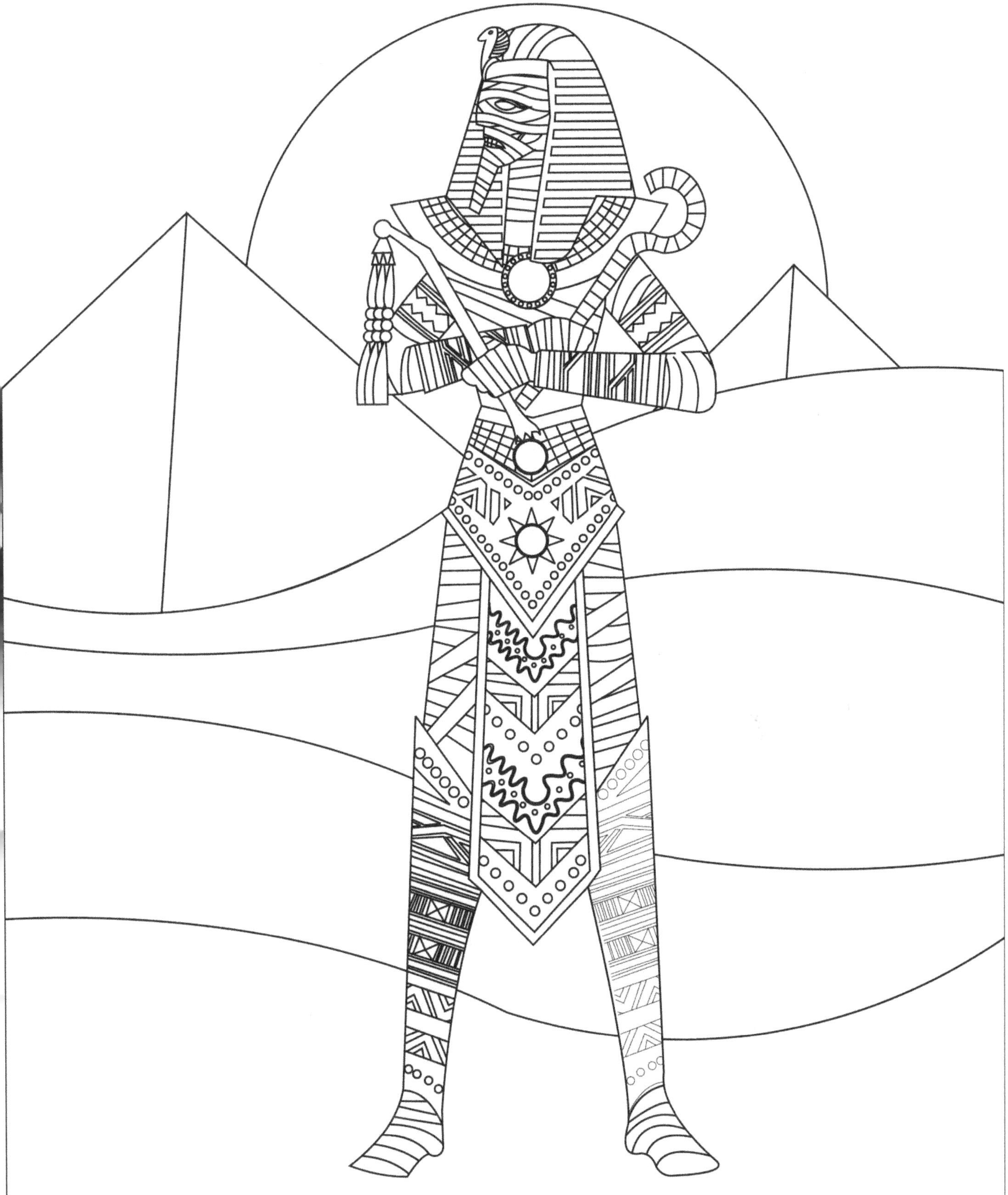

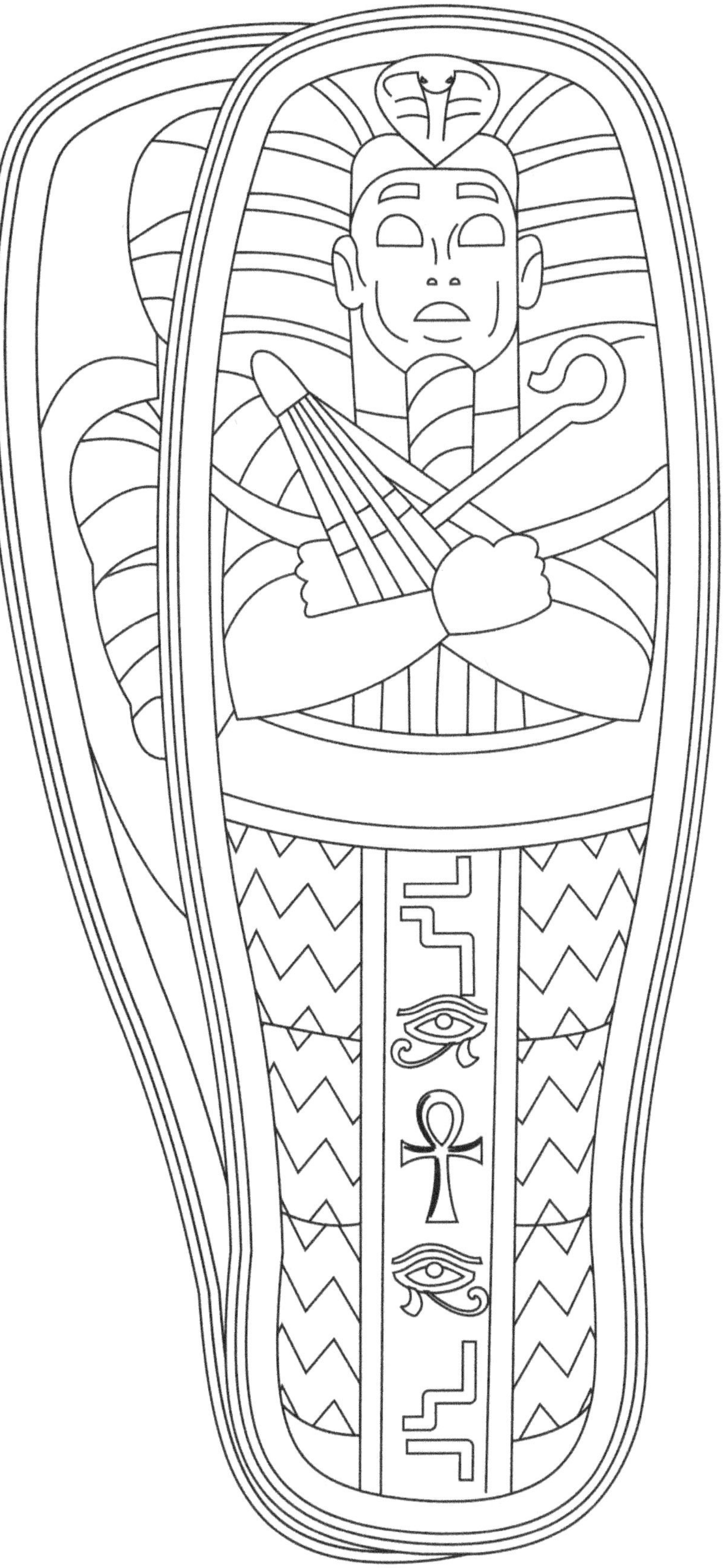

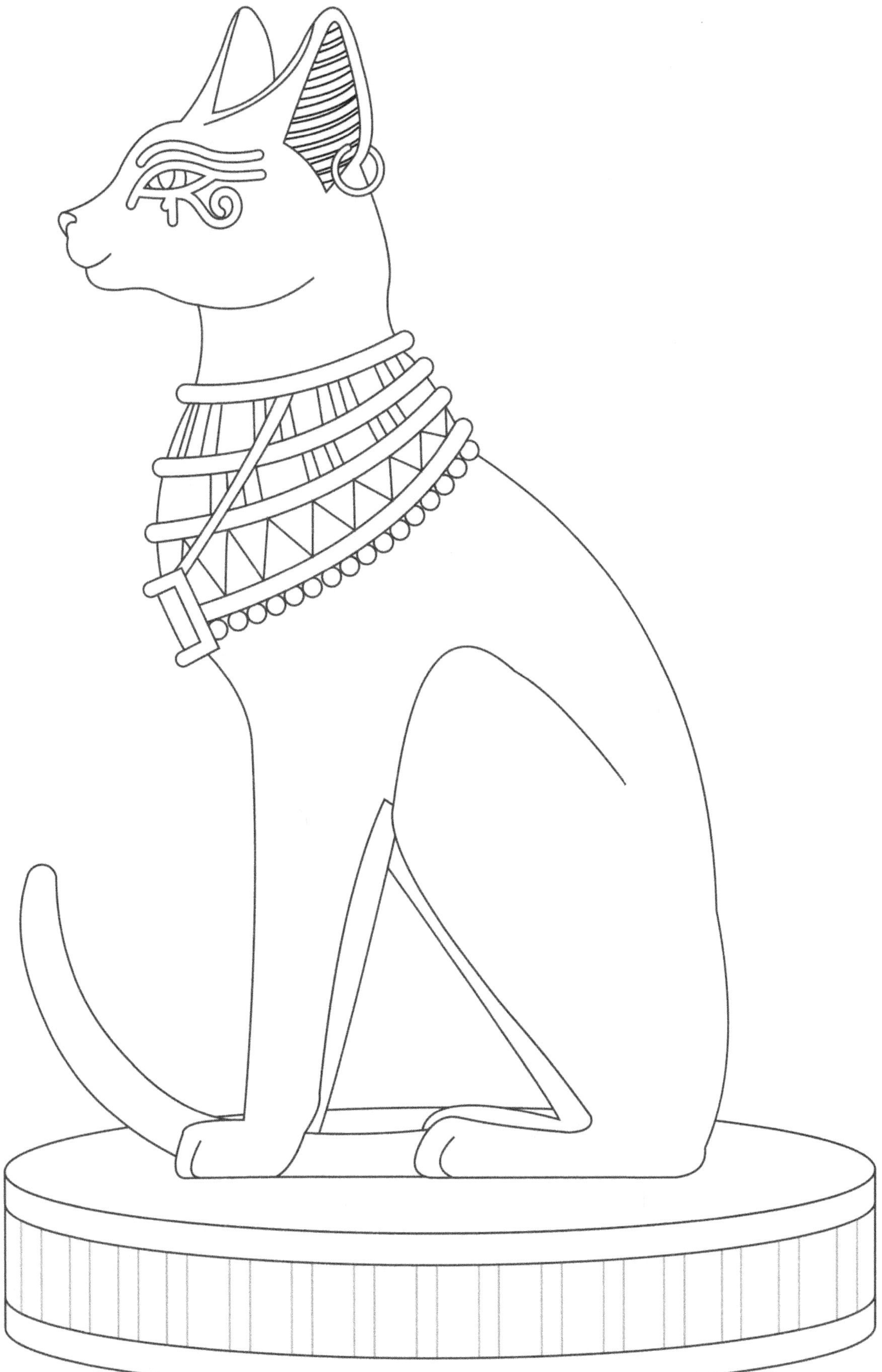

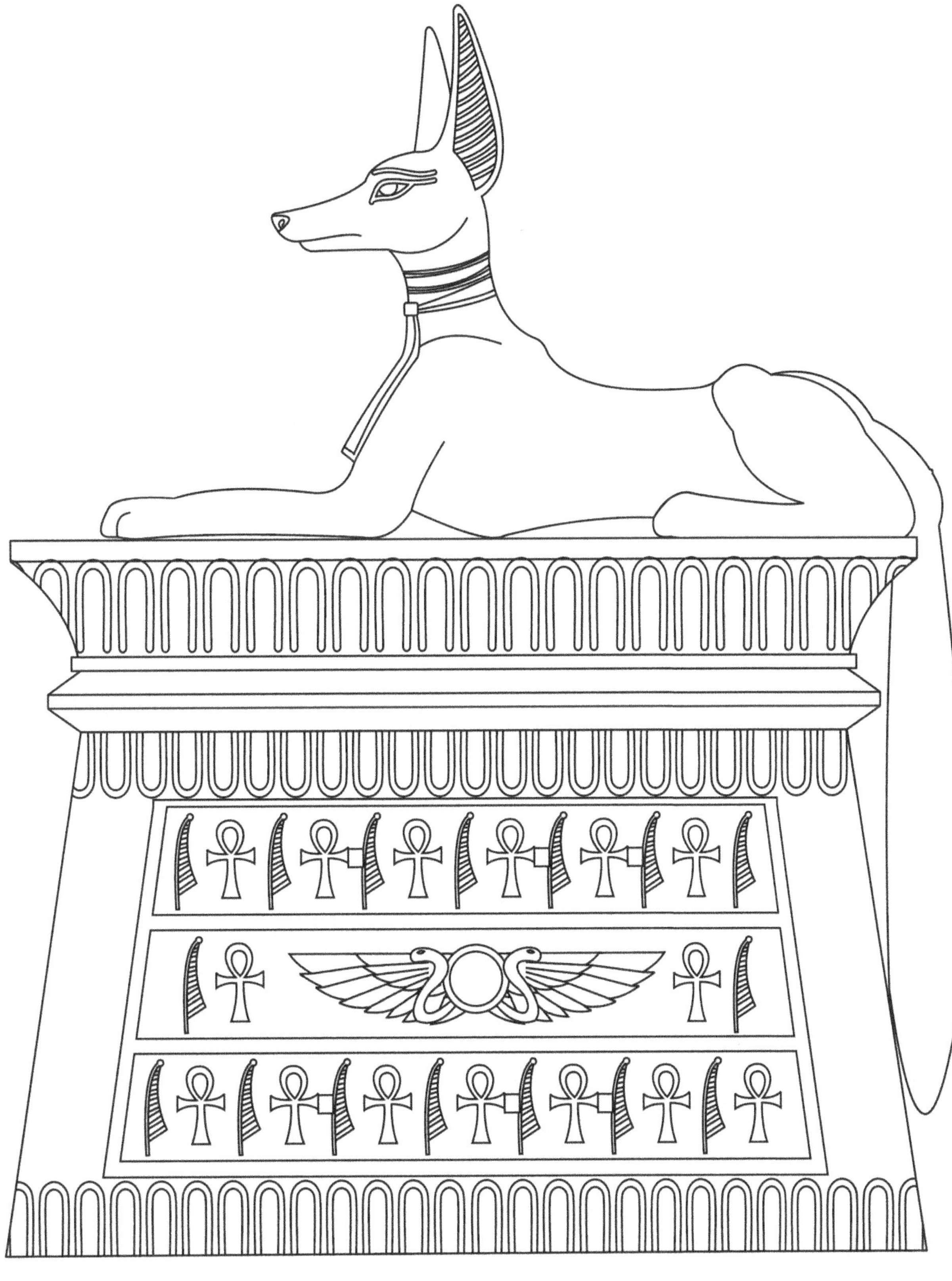

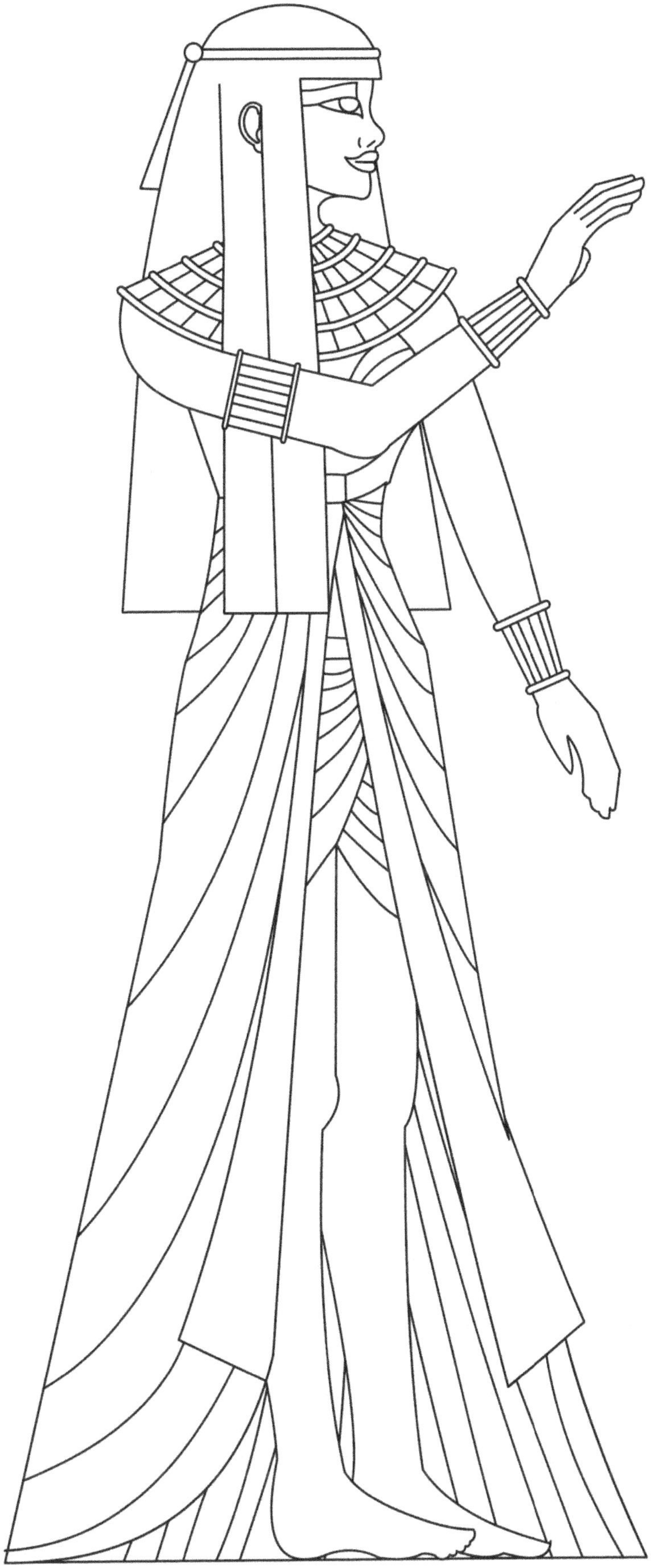

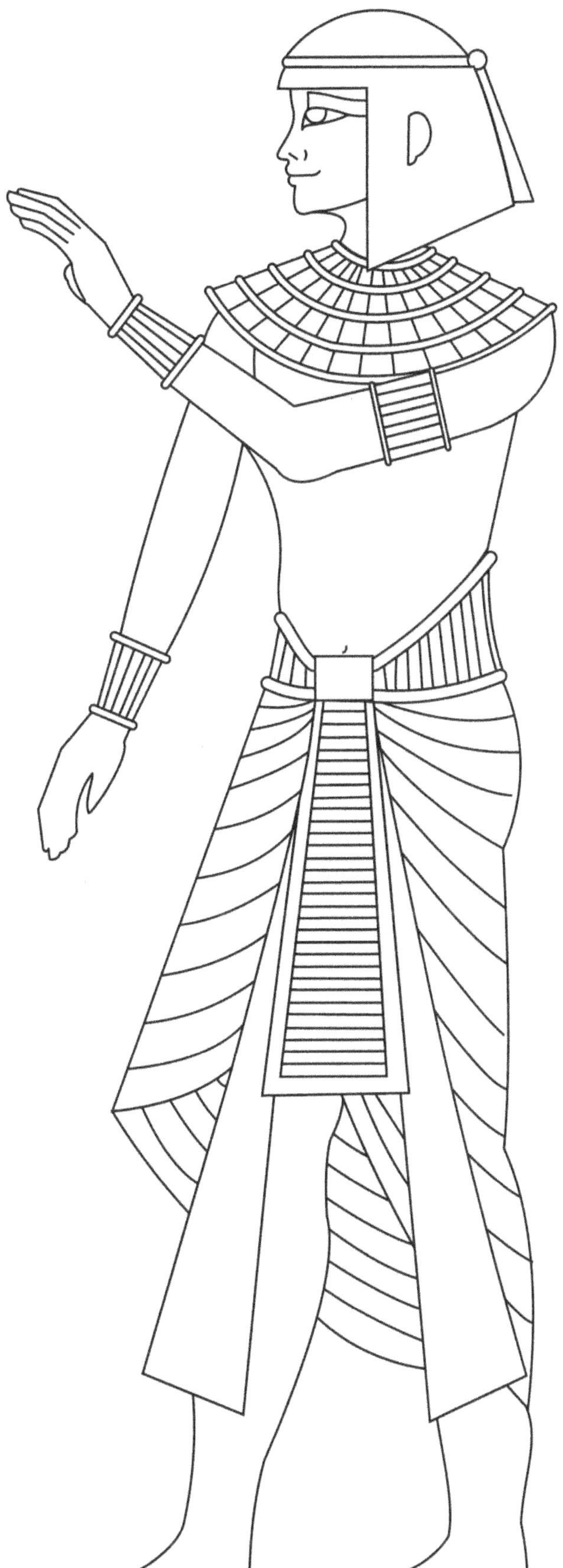

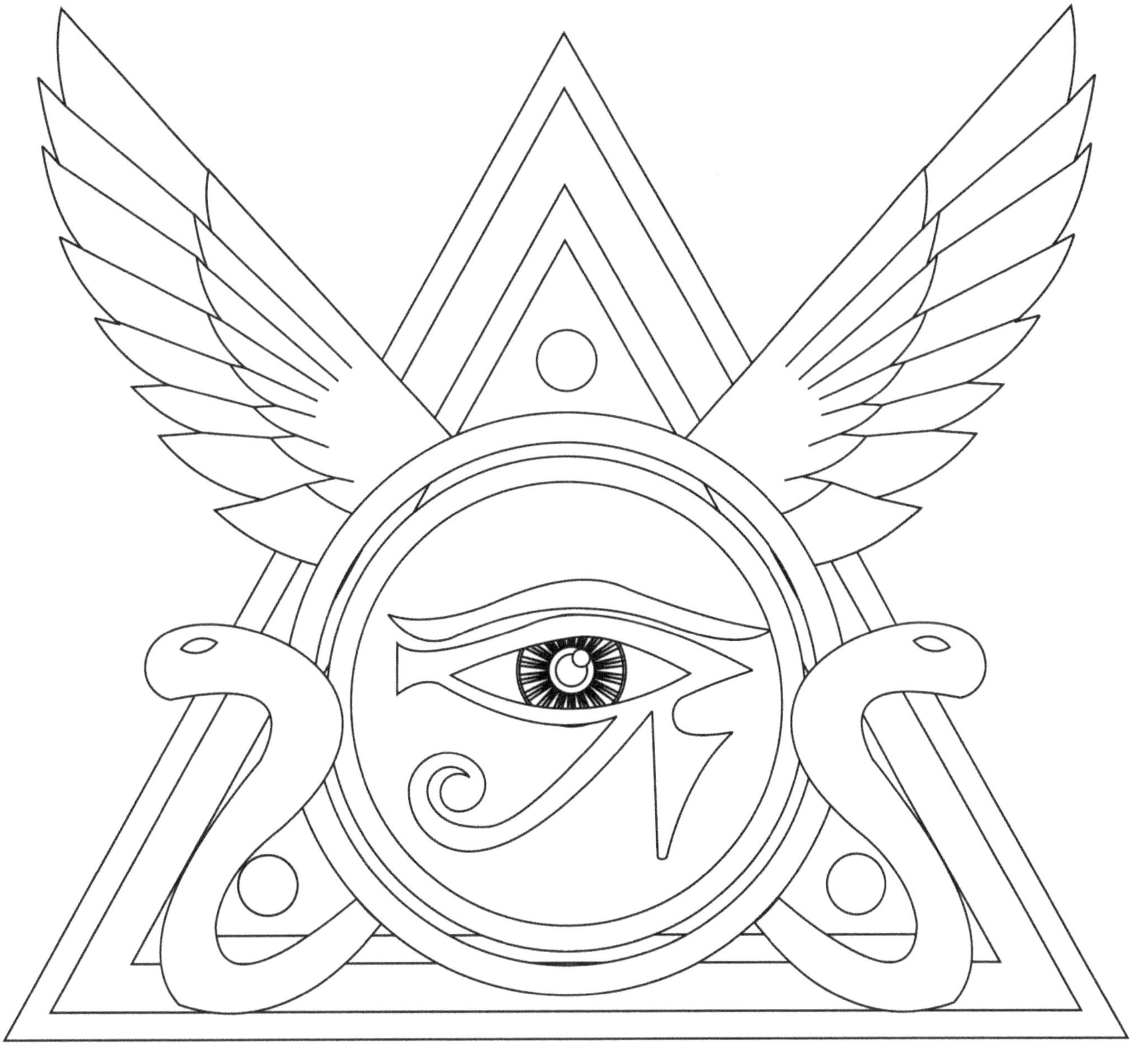

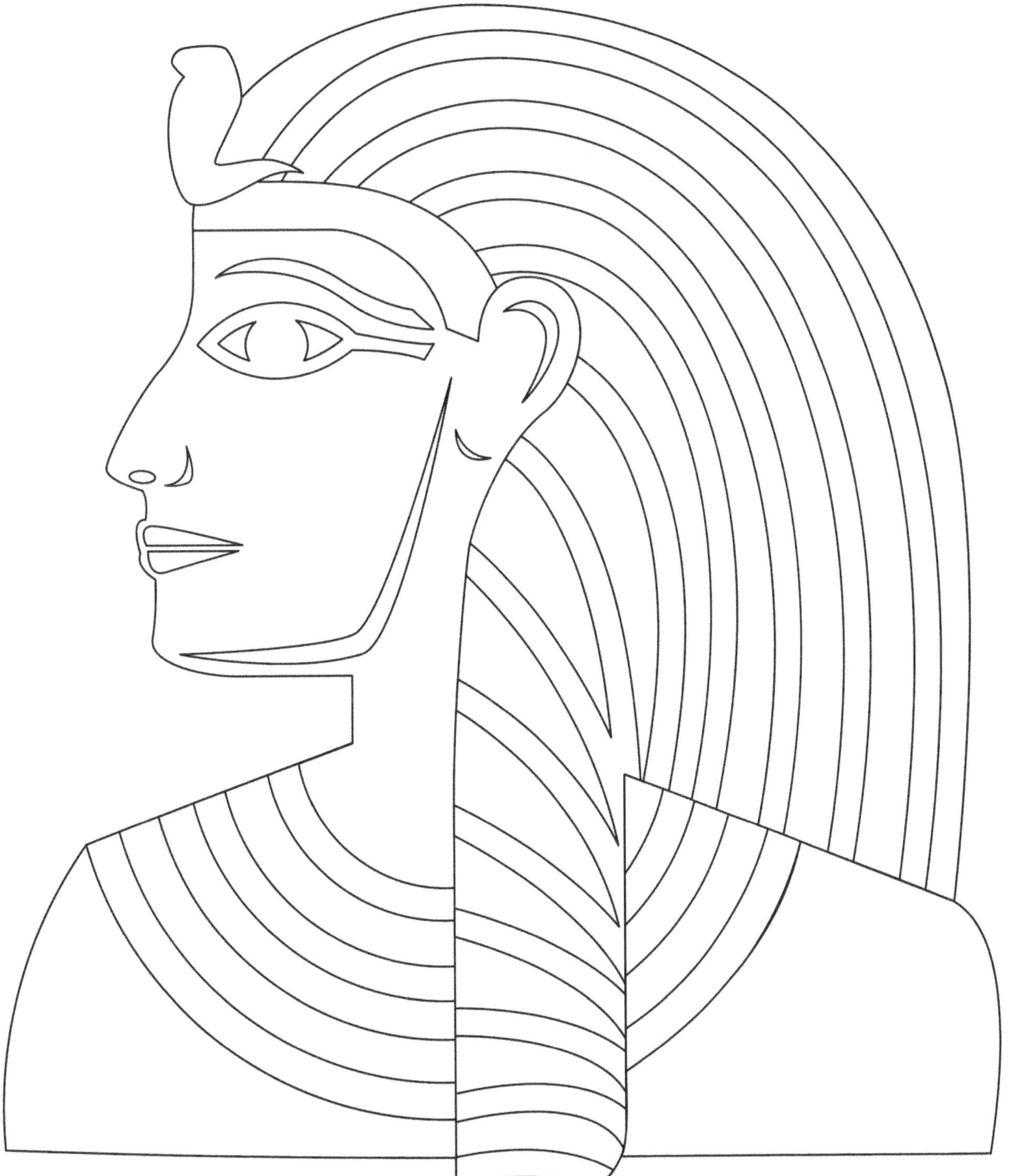

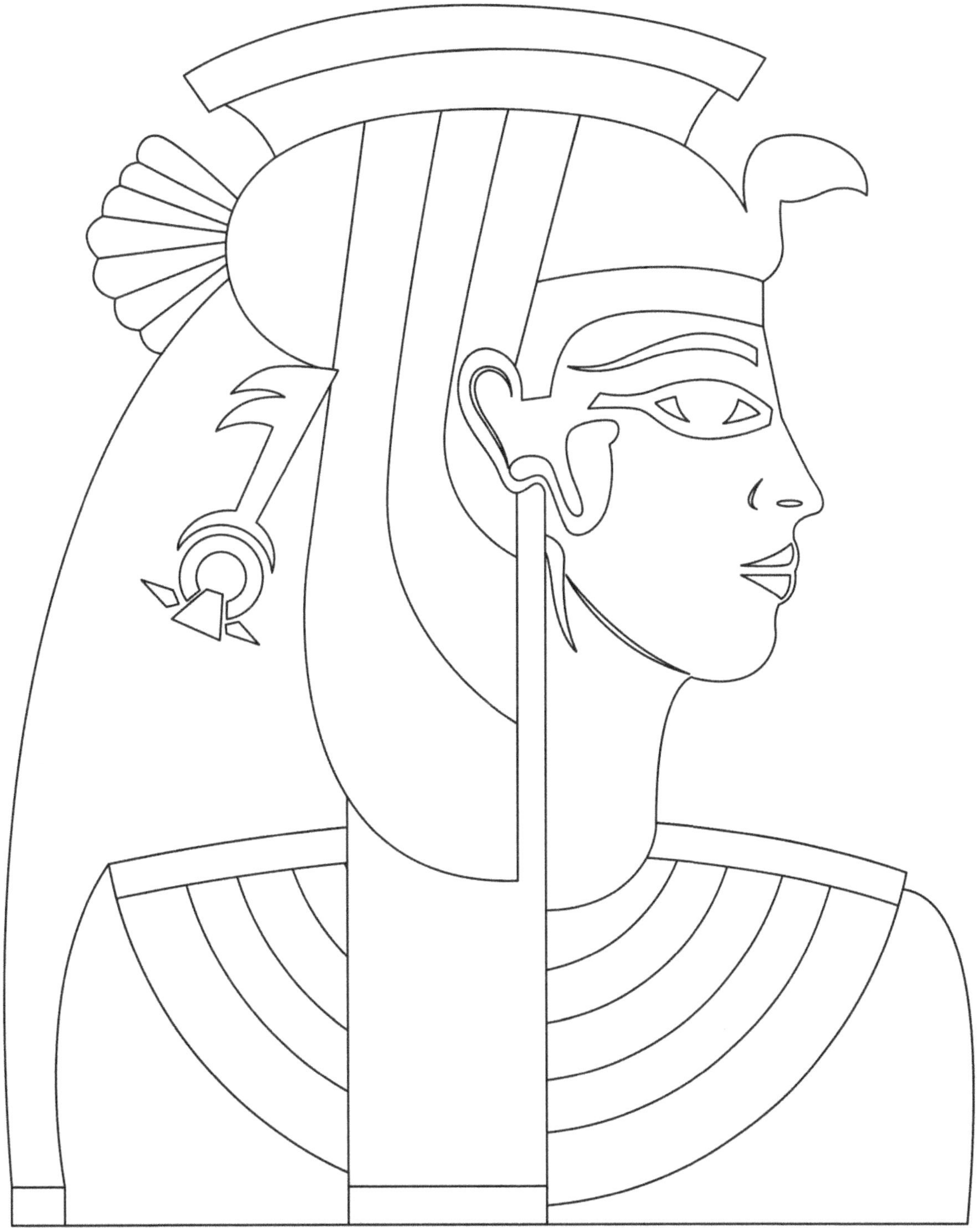

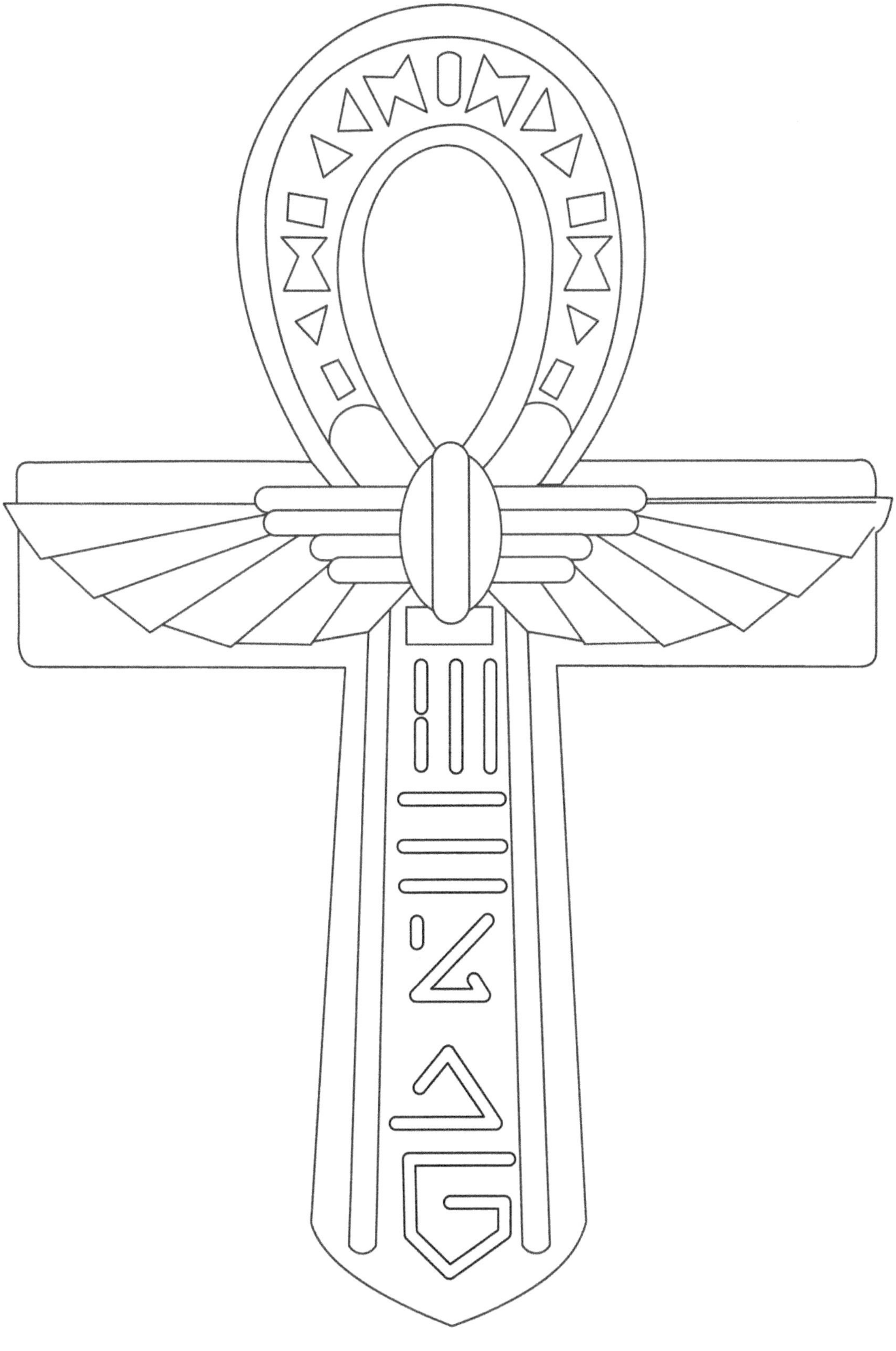

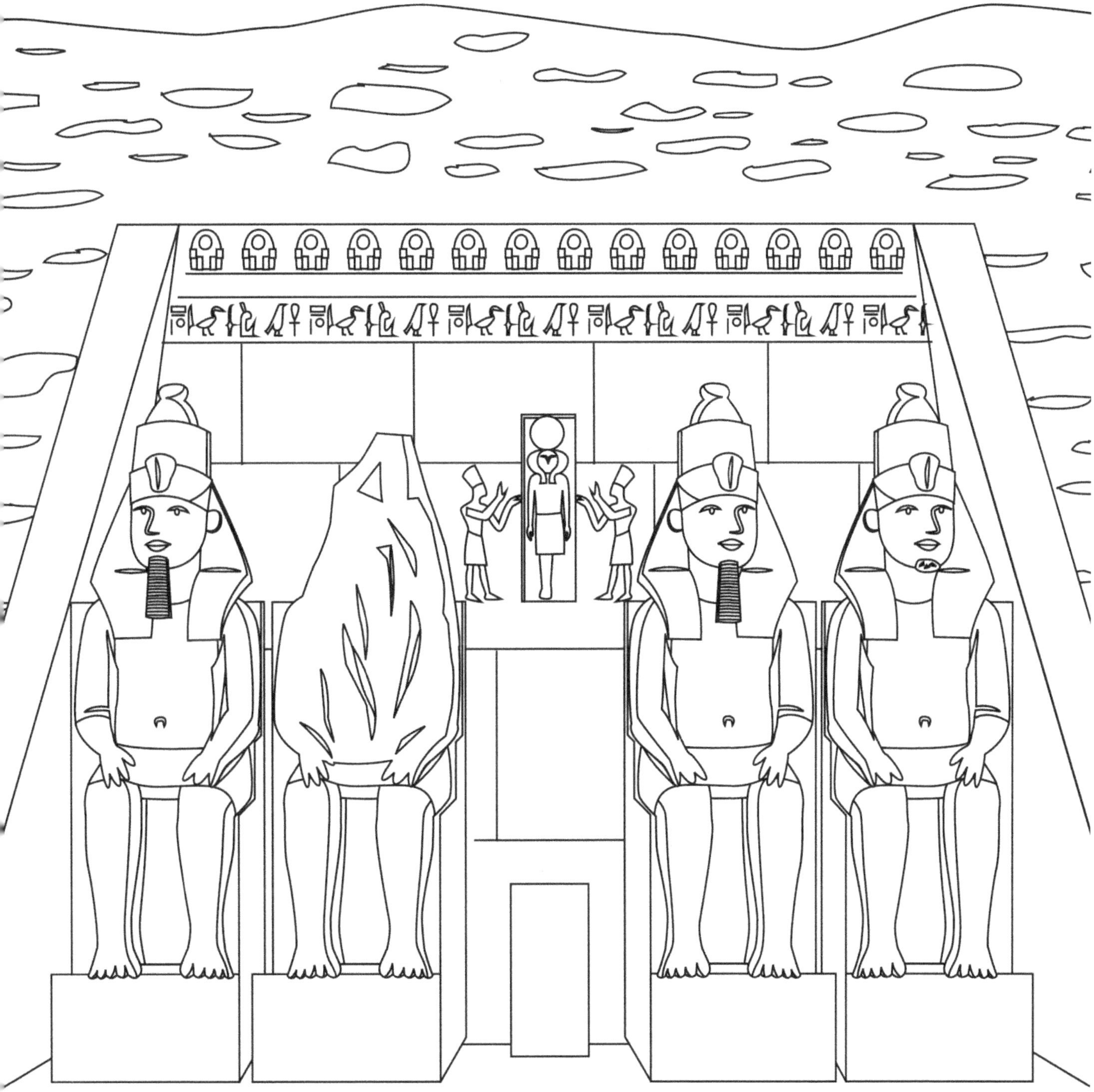

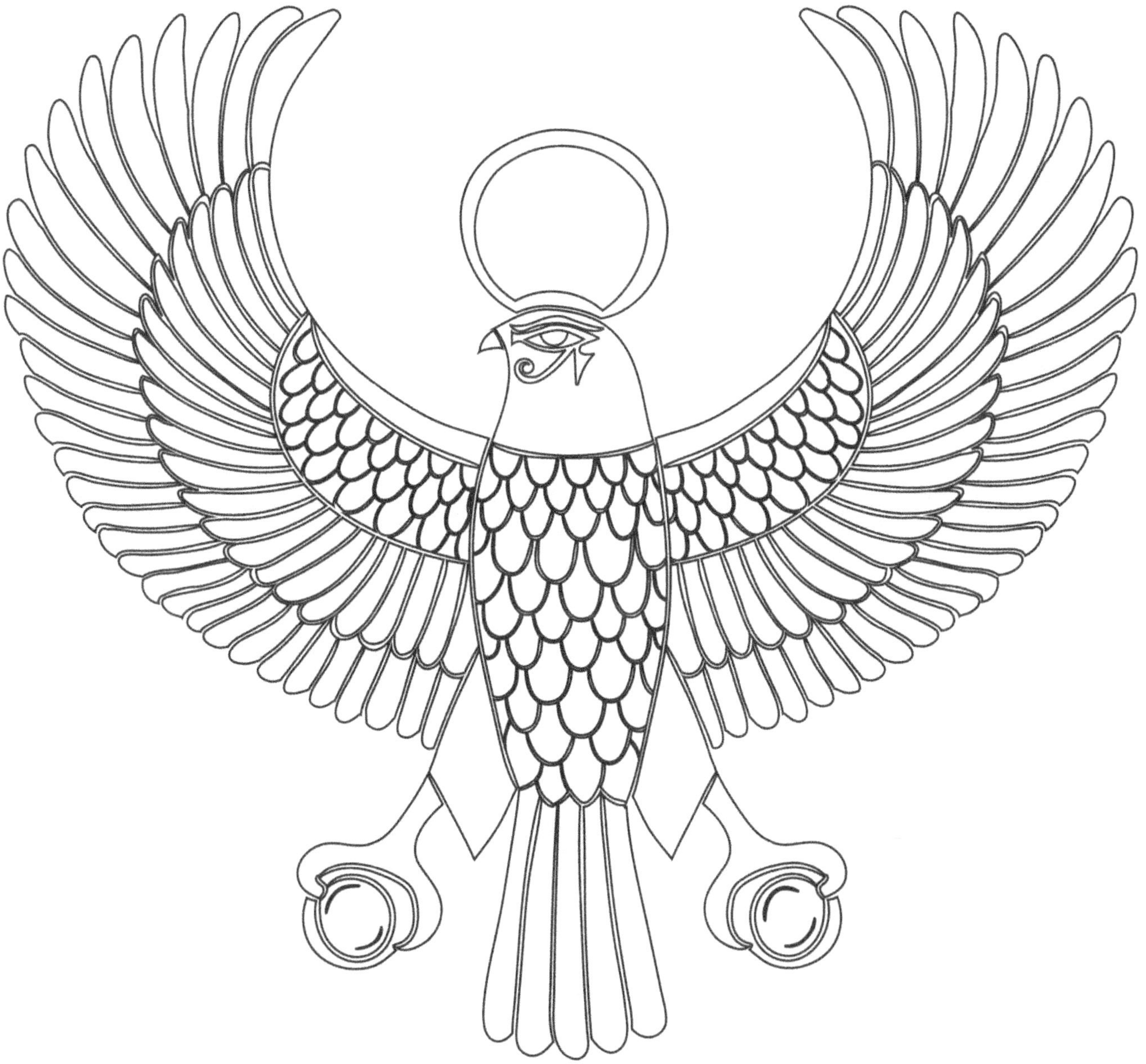

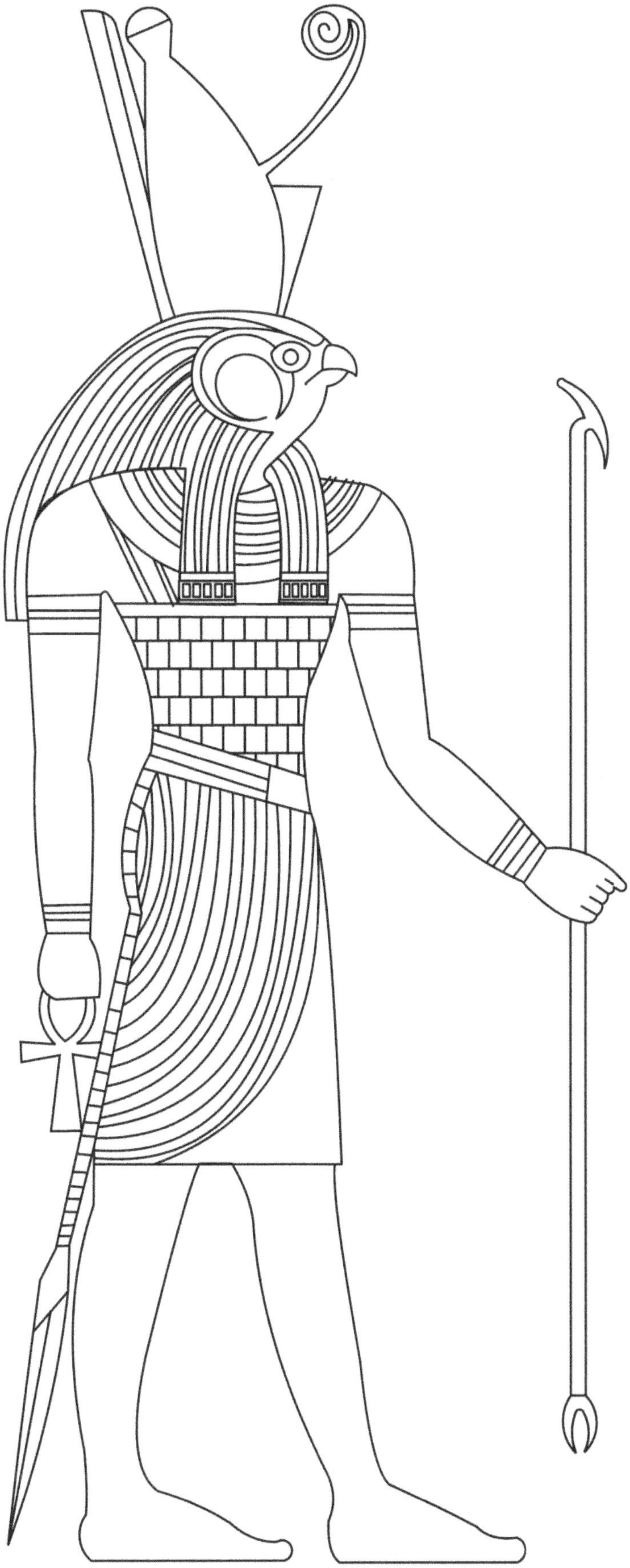

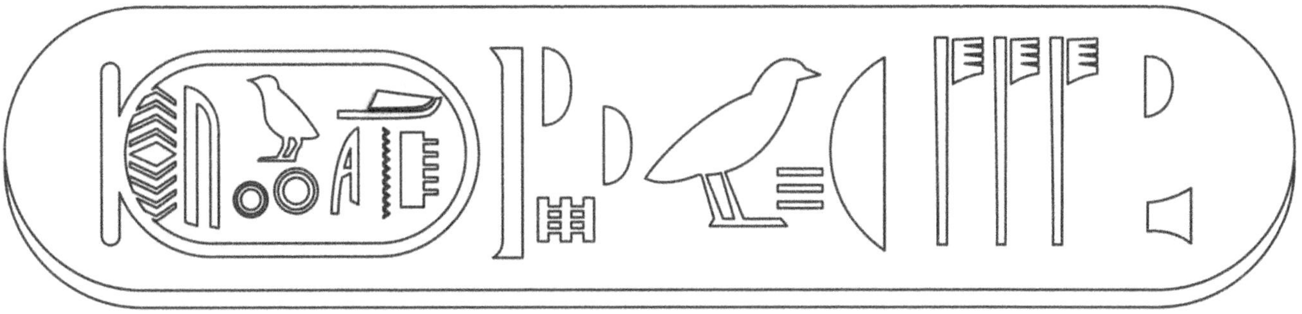

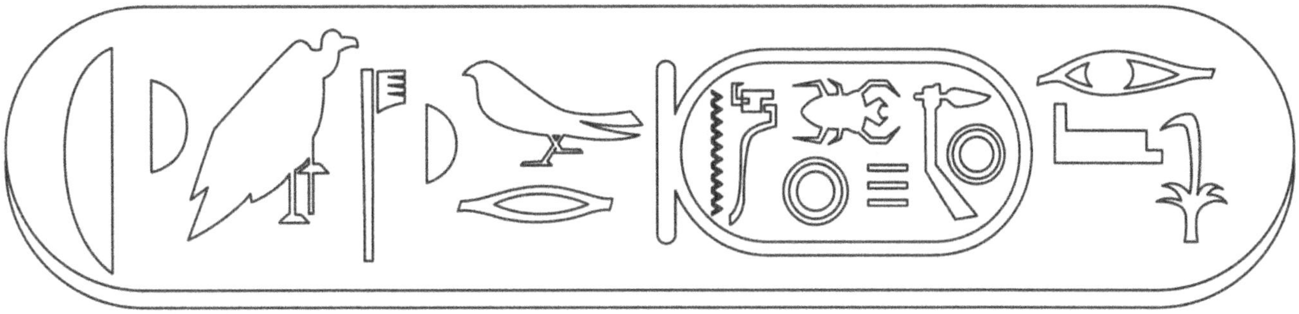

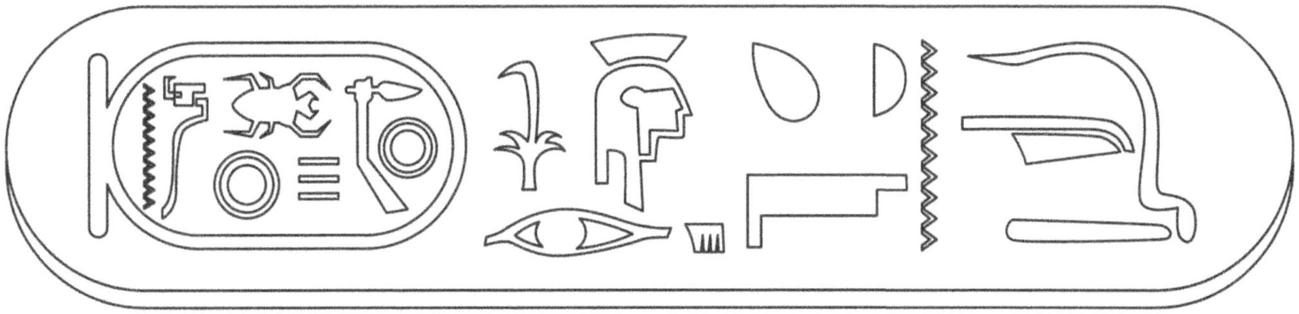

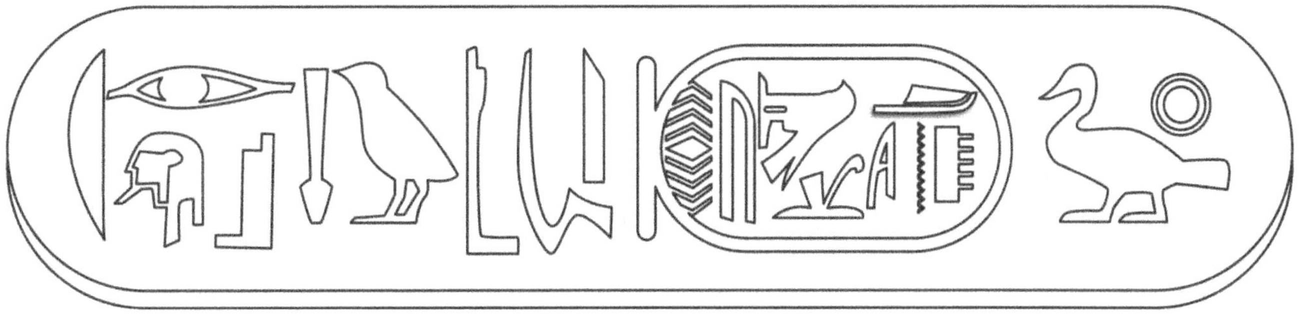

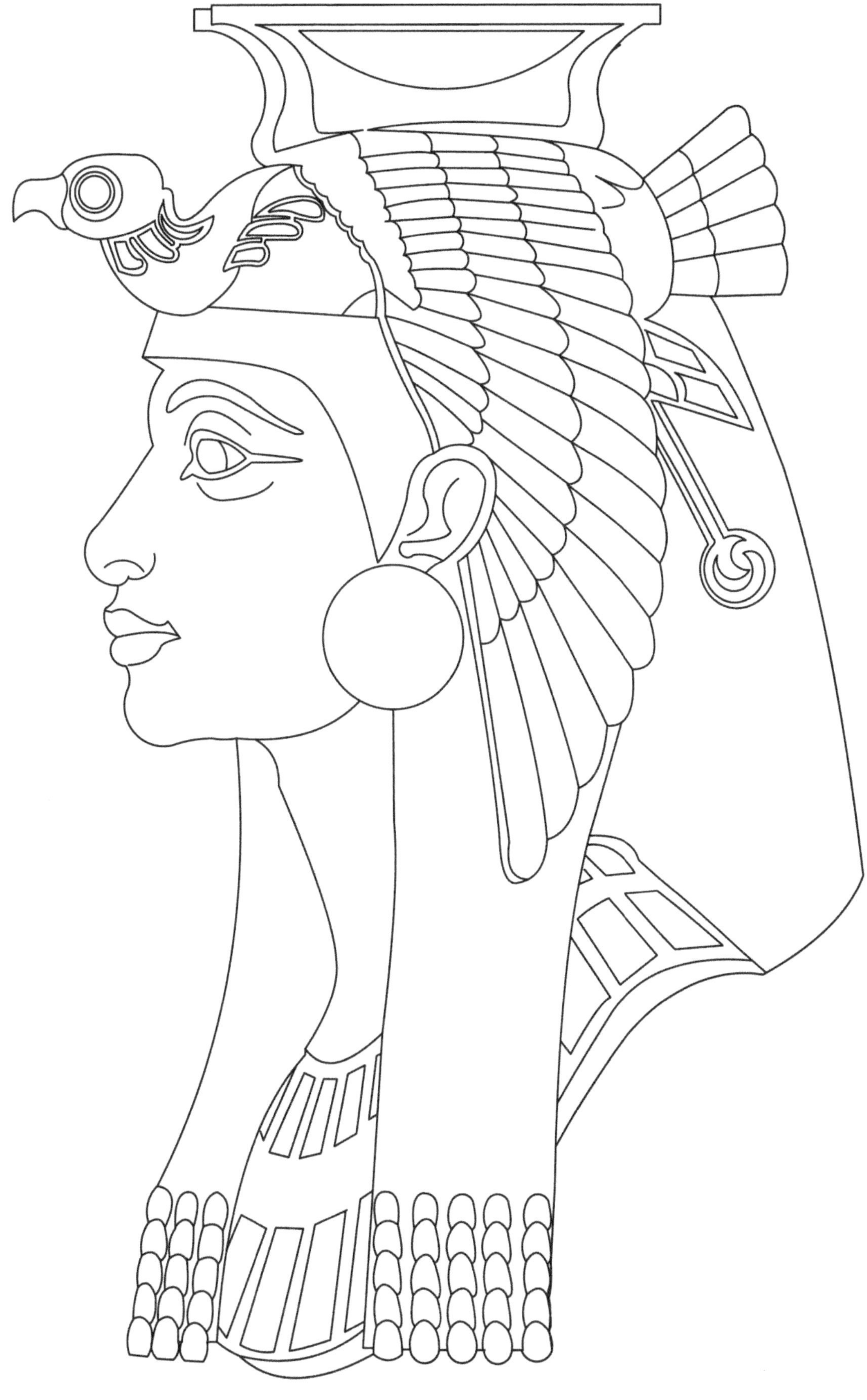

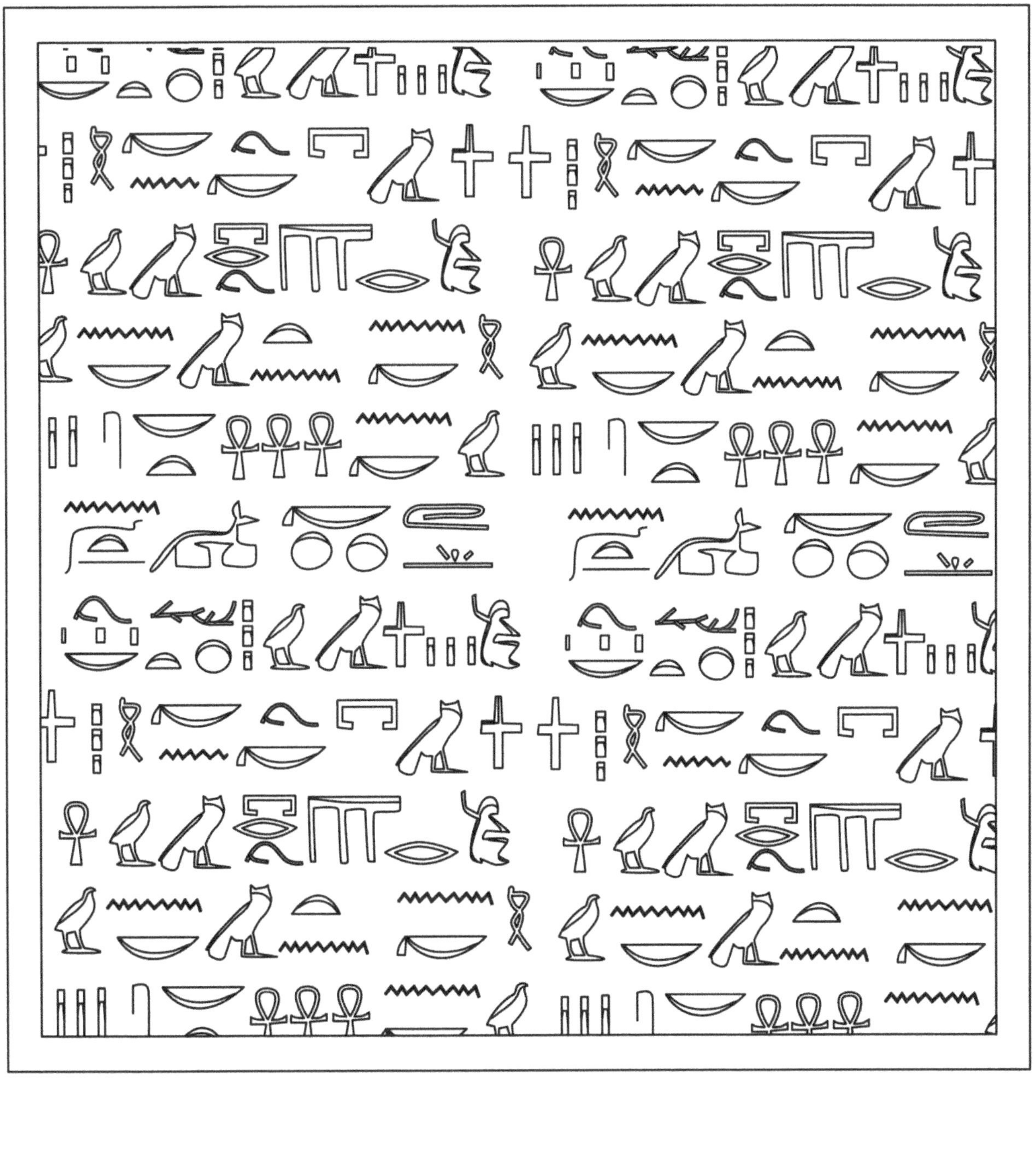

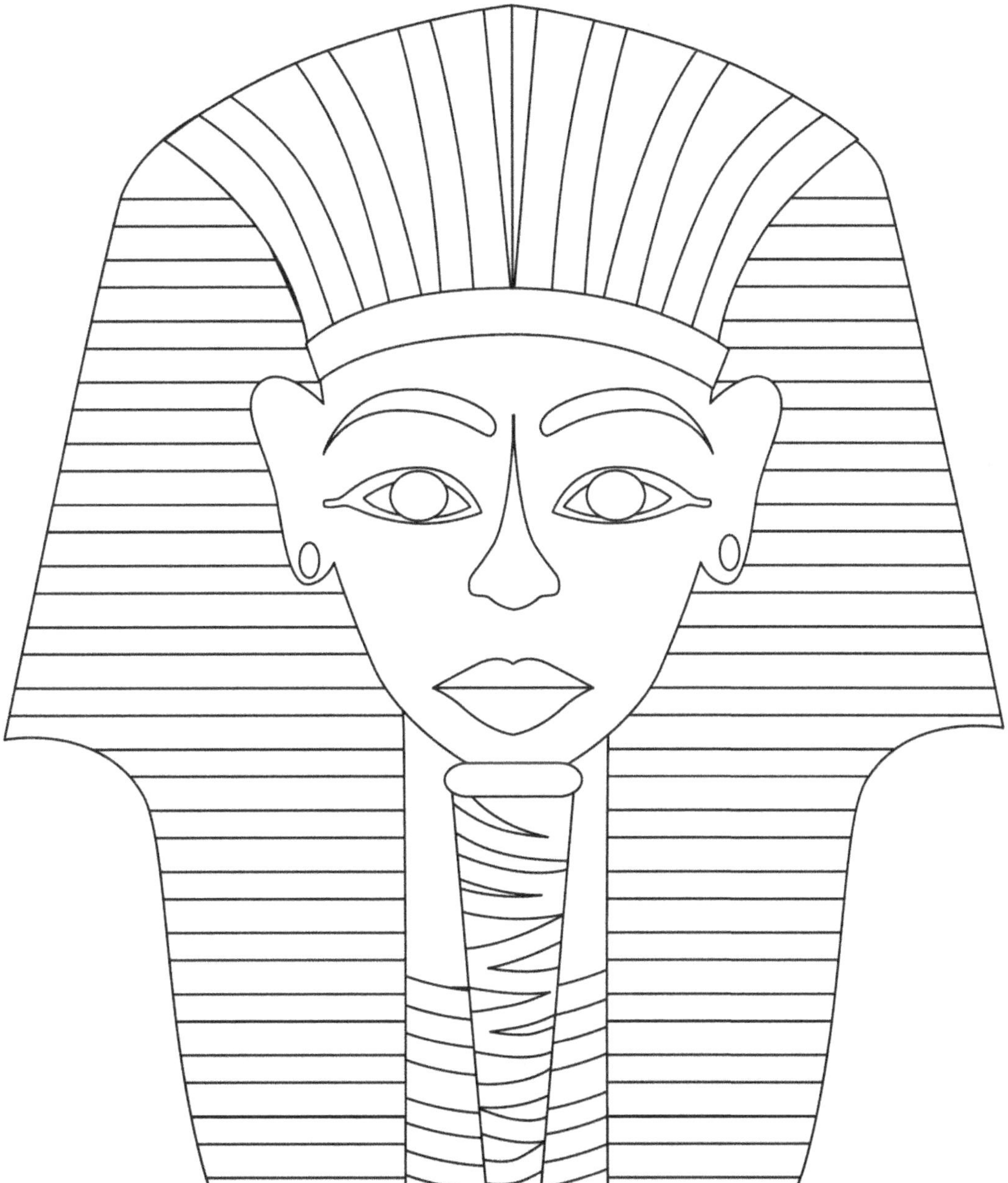

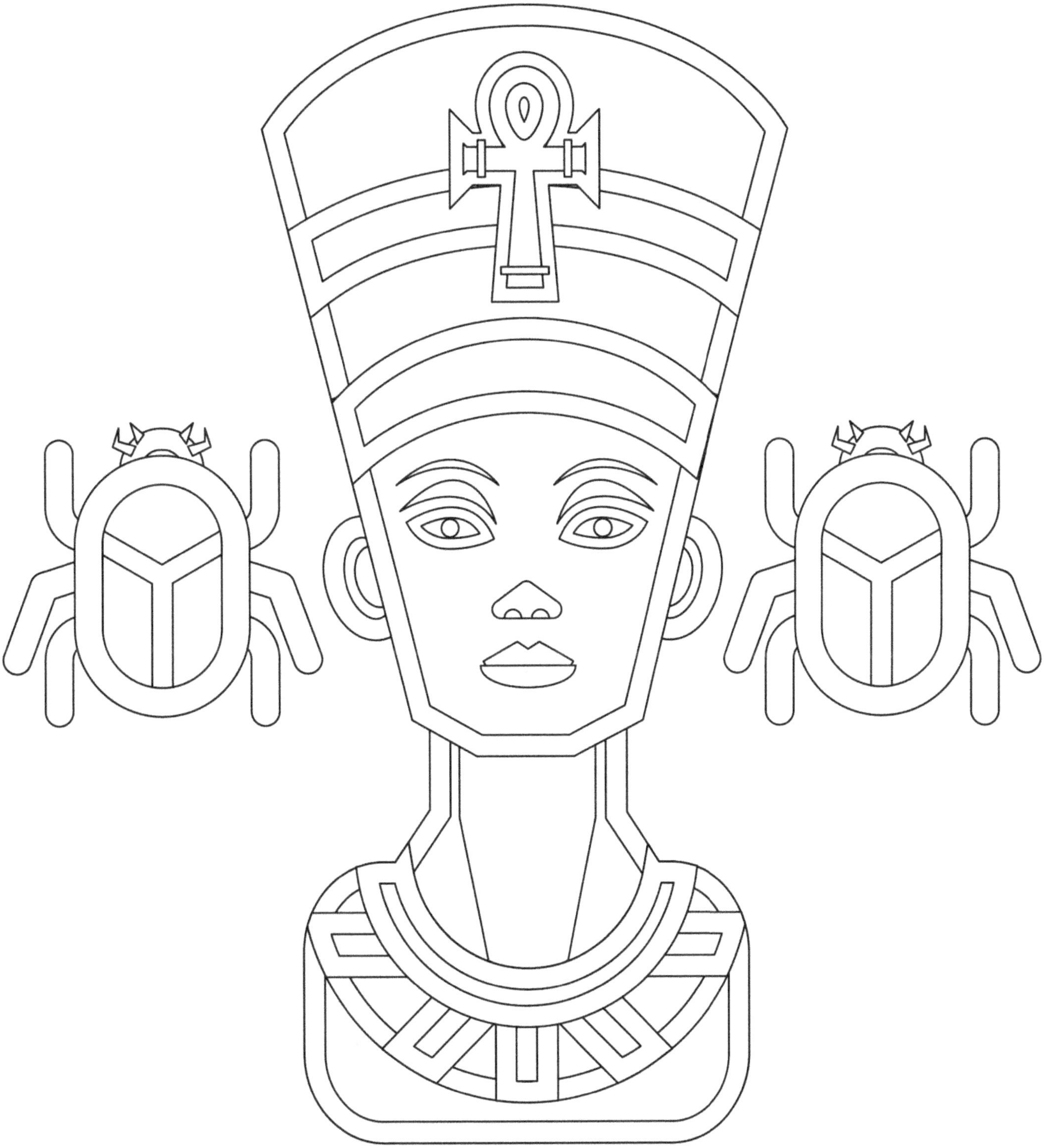

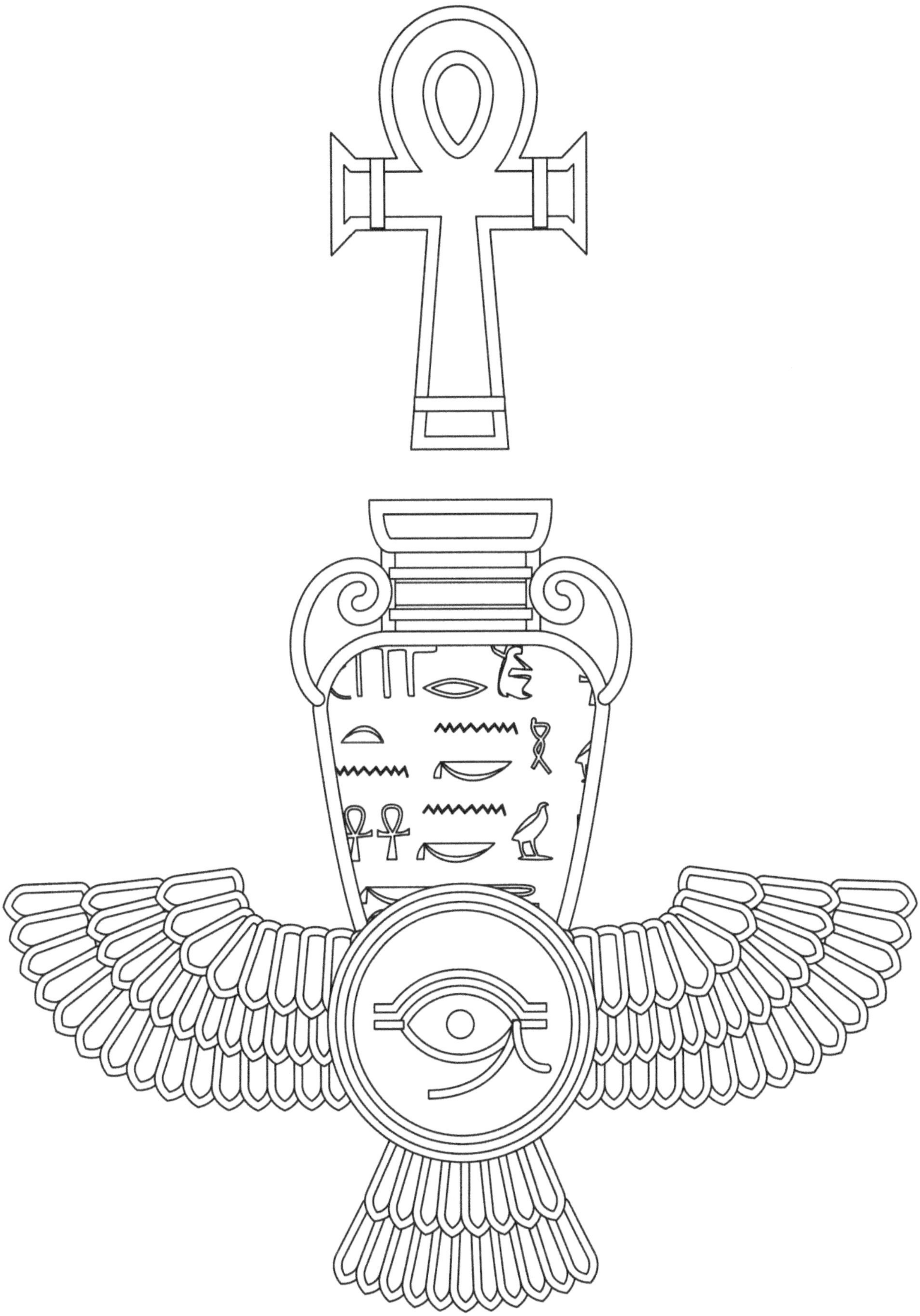

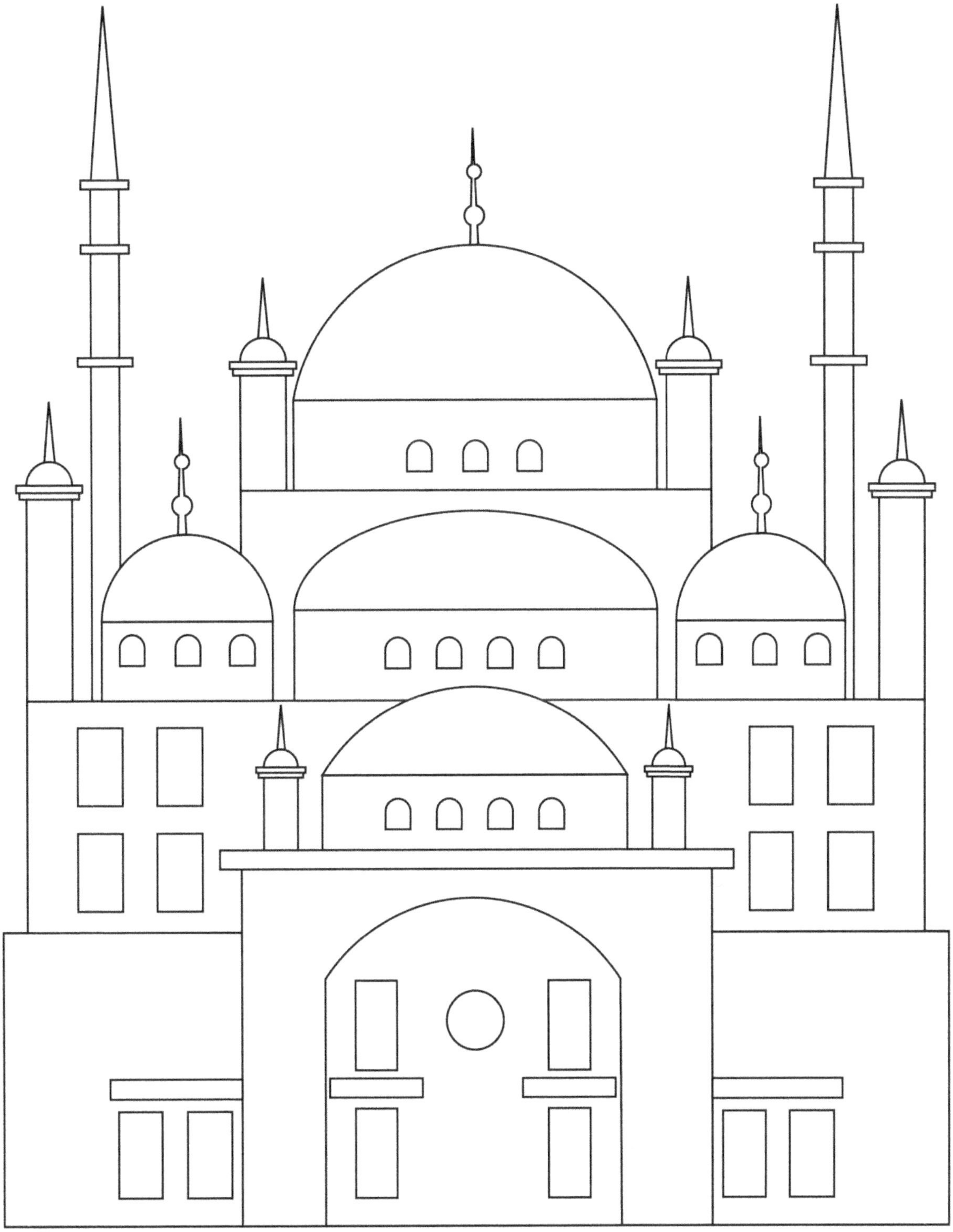

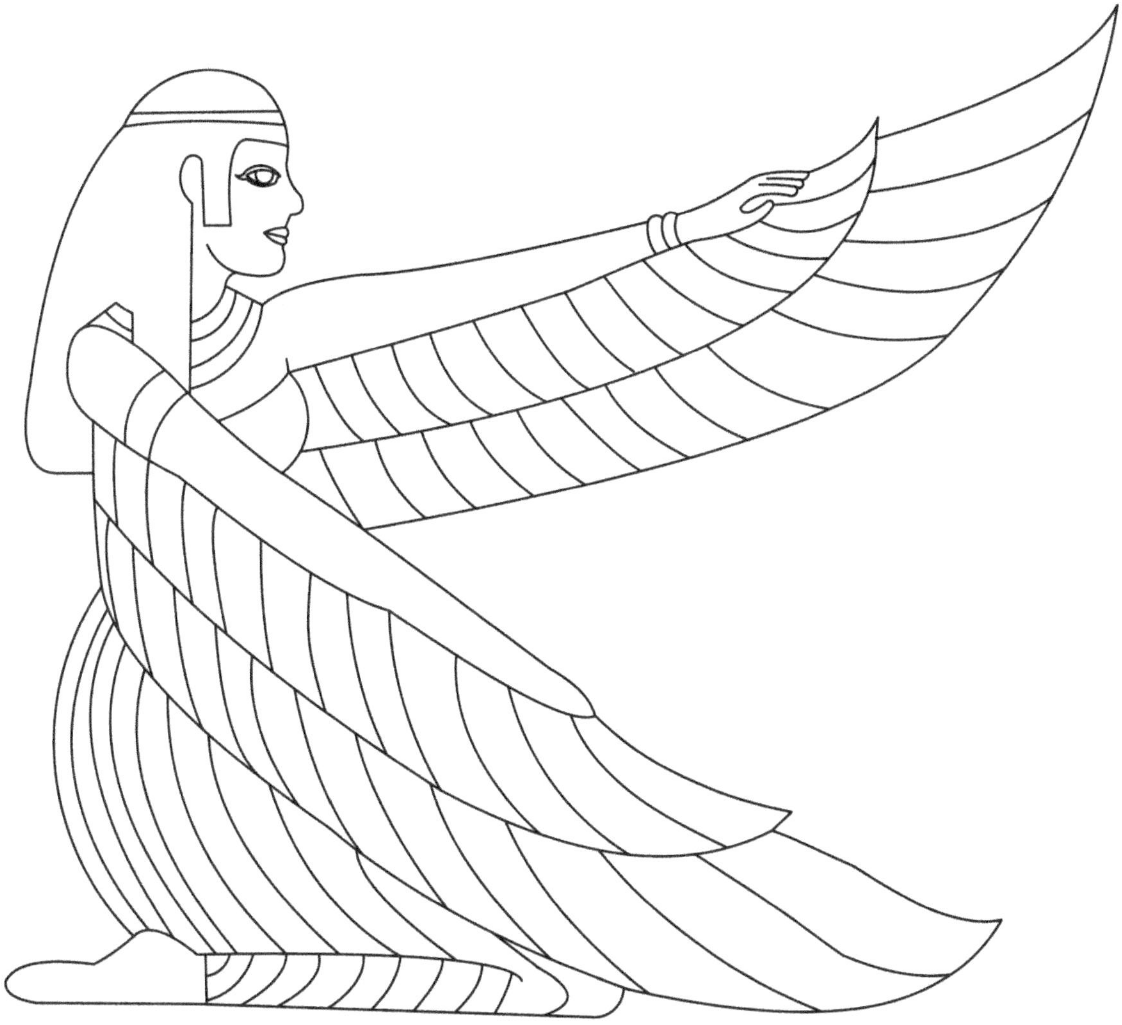

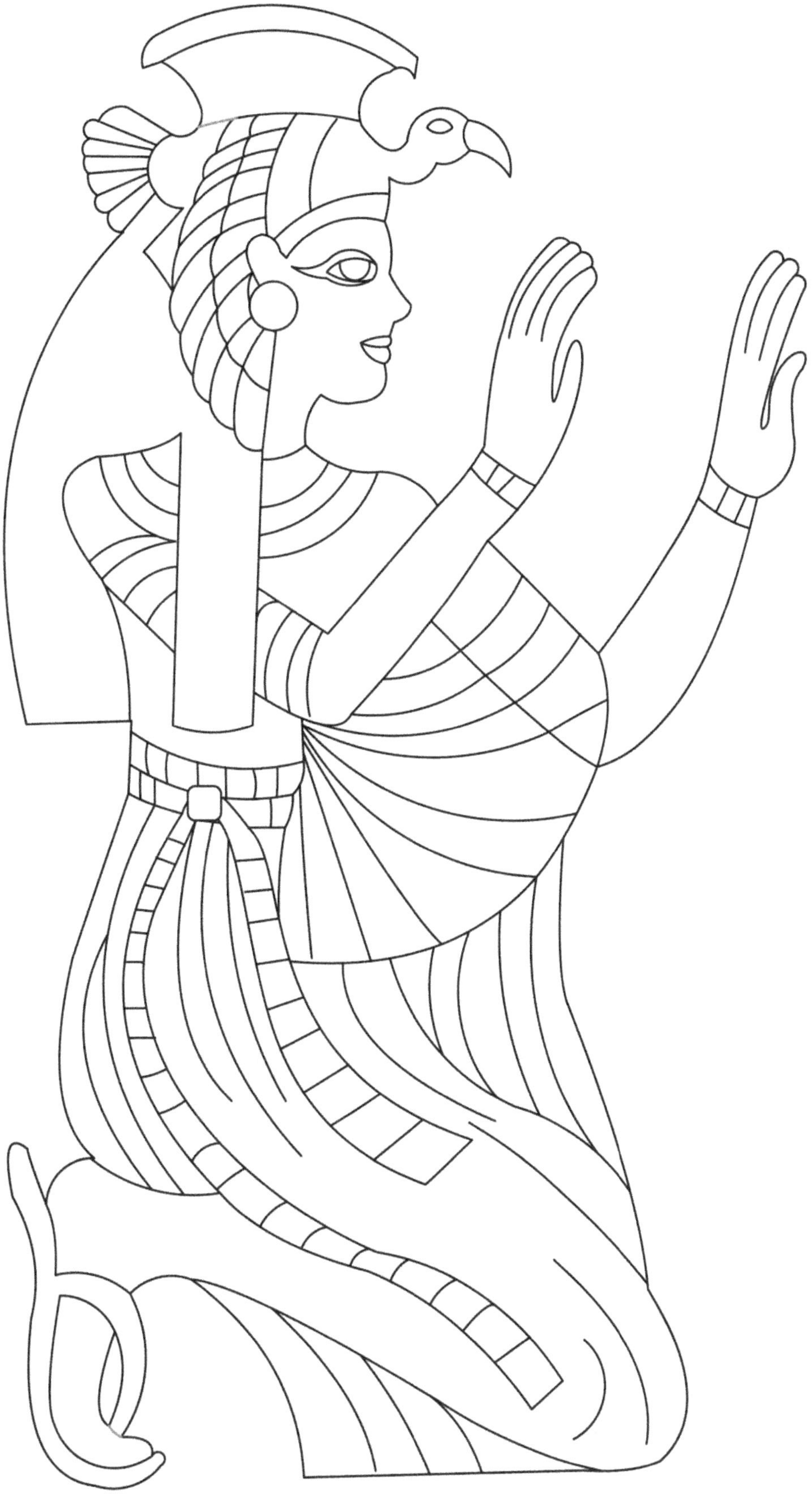

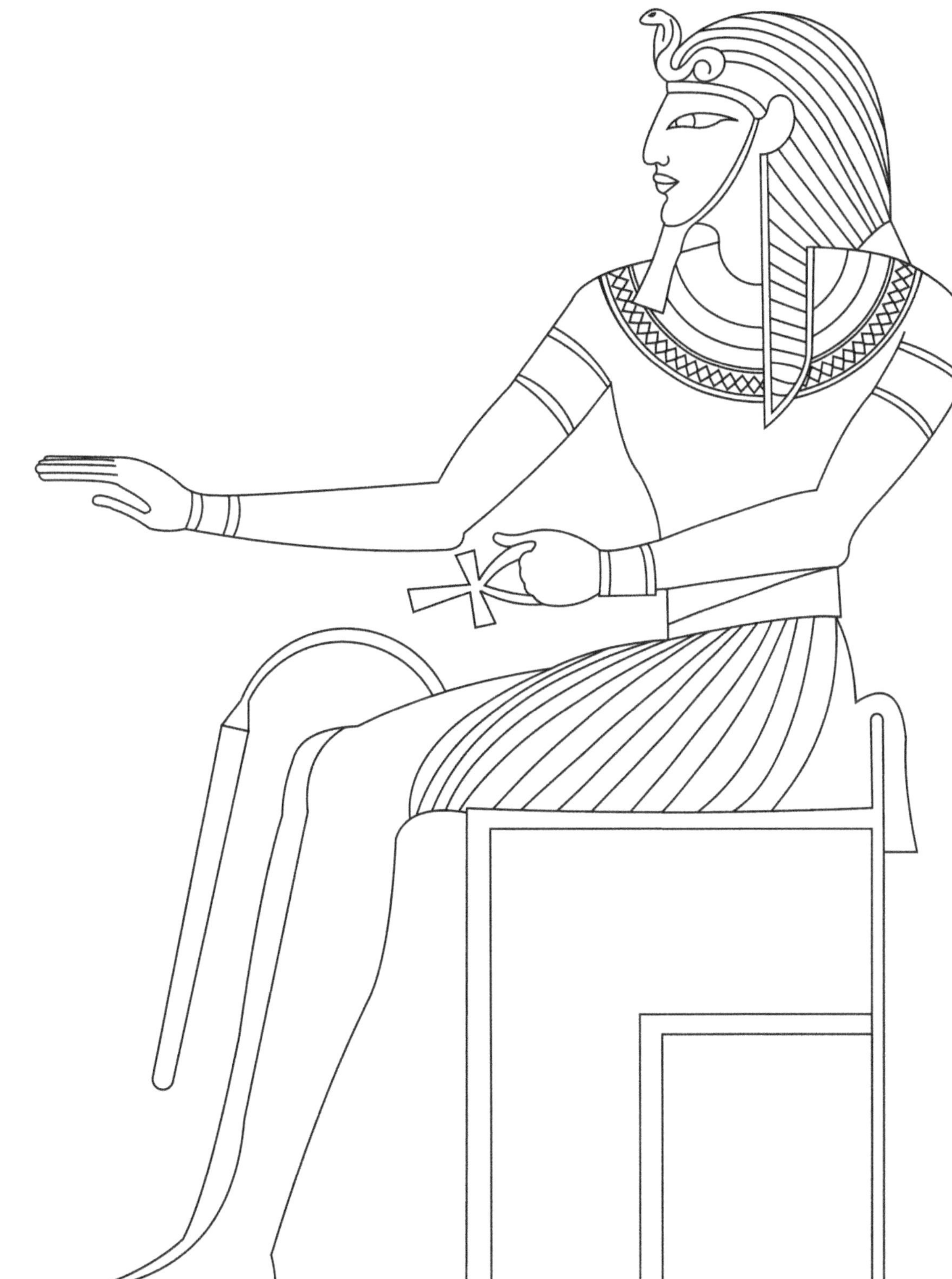

www.ingramcontent.com/pod-product-compliance
Lightning Source LLC
Chambersburg PA
CBHW082146230526
45467CB00043B/2303
* 9 7 8 1 7 1 7 3 9 7 1 5 7 *